RELIGION AND POLITICS

RELIGION AND POLITICS

Edited by

FRED E. BAUMANN

KENNETH M. JENSEN

Published for the Public Affairs Conference Center
Kenyon College
by the University Press of Virginia
Charlottesville

THE UNIVERSITY PRESS OF VIRGINIA
Copyright © 1989 by the Kenyon Public Affairs
Conference Center

Publication of this volume is sponsored by the Kenyon Public Affairs Conference
Center, Kenyon College, Gambier, Ohio. The authors alone are responsible for
the opinions expressed and any policies recommended in their respective papers.
The Kenyon Public Affairs Conference Center is a nonpartisan educational
program and as such takes no position on questions of public policy.

First published 1989

Library of Congress Cataloging-in-Publication Data
Religion and politics / edited by Fred E. Baumann, Kenneth M. Jensen.
   p. cm.
Papers from a conference held at Kenyon College by the Kenyon
Public Affairs Conference Center, Apr., 1985.
   Includes index.
   ISBN 0-8139-1199-0
   1. Religion and politics—Congresses.   2. Religion and politics—
United States—Congresses.   3. United States—Religion—Congresses.
I. Baumann, Fred E.   II. Jensen, Kenneth M. (Kenneth Martin) 1944–
III. Public Affairs Conference Center.
BL65.P7R4323   1989
322'.1'0973—dc19   88-34438
                                                                        CIP
Printed in the United States of America

Contents

Preface

Some years ago I worked for an organization of university professors led by a famous and elderly philosopher I had always admired and now was coming to revere. One hot Manhattan July afternoon he arrived in our shabby office in the Garment District looking a little bemused. Justly known for his courageous and untiring defense of human reason against every form of superstition, dogmatism, and barbarism the twentieth century had to lavish, he had just made his first contact with the "Jews for Jesus." One of them, he told me, was a girl who couldn't have been more than sixteen. "I asked her," he said, "'Does your mother know what you're doing?'"

His question, it occurred to me later, might stand for the bemusement of many of us for whom the ultimate dominance of secular standards in public affairs had seemed, whether for good or ill, a settled question not too long ago when we were confronted by the revived and newly confident claim to authority of a wide, not to say bewildering, array of religious perspectives. For while revivals of churchgoing, à la the 1950s, were unsurprising and even new bursts of religious enthusiasm as such seemed expectable, there was something unawaited in the assurance with which religiously based claims were put forth in public debate. And that rediscovered assurance raised afresh some very important questions.

Setting aside any world-historical speculations about the need for faith even (or especially) of societies enlightened by natural science, the eagerness of religious Americans to enter the public lists in the name of religious truth (whether against abortion or the government of El

Salvador, whether for school prayer or SWAPO), raised again the double question that had been very much a live issue for the founders of this nation. First, what kind of acknowledgment and respect can religions, which derive their certainty from divine revelation, give to a liberal democracy which, at a minimum, lacks such certainty? Second, what kind of acknowledgment and respect can liberal democracy give to religions and to religion as such?

Frederick Schauer's article looks at this double question from the viewpoint of the state by examining the establishment clause of the First Amendment. His argument for maintaining a wall of separation between church and state while allowing a few prudent cracks at once illustrates the issues at stake in translating any constitutional principle into public policy, but it also illuminates the particular tensions inherent in a society in which there is both great support for religion and a consent to limit its claims in the public realm.

The essays of Father Robert Drinan and Father Ernest Fortin seem naturally juxtaposed. Not only do they debate the claim of a particular set of teachings about social justice within one religious tradition—Roman Catholicism—but, perhaps more importantly, they explore the very possibility of translating a personal religious conviction into a system of policy preferences. It should be evident that this latter issue extends far beyond one given religious tradition to most if not all religiously based claims to prescribe for the public good.

Werner Dannhauser's essay is addressed not to a particular religious tradition so much as to a political one. It warns conservatives, who often consider themselves the allies of religion, against misusing religion by domesticating it into a tame supporter of their policies. But parallel and obverse to Father Fortin's essay, Dannhauser's argument calls up to us the vast gulf between the ultimate concerns of revelation and those of liberal democratic politics. Yet, writing out of yet another tradition, that of evangelical Protestantism, Jerry Combee responds by asserting the common origins of liberal democracy and religion in acceptance of the paramount claim of individual conscience. Finally, Peter Ahrensdorf invokes the most exotic perspective of the book, that of ancient Greek political philosophy, in order to meditate on how religion is seen by founders of regimes (and by their teachers) who are themselves not operating from religious assumptions. His essay can, it seems to me, be read in parallel, though at a much different level, with Frederick Schauer's, since both look at religion from without.

This volume emerges from a conference held in April 1985 under the auspices of the Kenyon Public Affairs Conference Center at Kenyon College. The first four essays were written for the conference, the fifth was composed by a conference participant in response to the discussions, and the sixth was commissioned subsequently for inclusion in this volume.

We gratefully acknowledge our indebtedness to the supporters of the PACC, the Earhart Foundation, Murch Division of Parker/Hunter, Inc., the Alfred P. Sloan Foundation, and the Exxon Foundation, whose generosity enables the PACC to carry on its work. The editors are deeply obligated to Sheryl A. Furniss, administrative assistant of the Kenyon Public Affairs Conference Center, and to Judy Sacks, who helped prepare the volume.

FRED E. BAUMANN
with KENNETH M. JENSEN

RELIGION AND POLITICS

Forcing, Enforcing, and Reinforcing:
The Problem of Religion and the State

FREDERICK SCHAUER

For someone accustomed to thinking about the subject of church and state under the rubric of "religion and the law," the designation for this volume—*Religion and Politics*—presents an important contrast. For we think of politics as the science of the possible and also, in a broadly majoritarian society, as the science of public opinion as it affects and is affected by official power. To a lawyer this suggests that the relevant law must be looked at in its political, social, cultural, and behavioral context. This is an immense topic, of course, but perhaps it can be narrowed somewhat by focusing on a number of more particular questions. What is the relationship between the legal norm and human behavior, both before and after enforcement of that norm? Is there congruence, or even correlation, between what the norm requires and what people actually do? Is the relationship between the norm and actual behavior in part a function of the relationship between the norm and the preexisting views of those to whom the norm is addressed? Similarly, what is the relationship between the legal norm and public opinion, again both before and after enforcement of that norm? Again, is there congruence, or even correlation, between what the norm commands and what people actually believe? And finally, what is the relationship between public opinion and the enforceability of the norm?

I take these as central issues in thinking about law generally and about a large number of specific substantive legal topics. But I take this array of political and behavioral issues as even more central in thinking about law and religion, because we are here confronted with a tension as striking as that existing anywhere in the exercise of official power. On the one hand we have the legal norm that finds its expression in the establishment clause of the First Amendment[1]—separation of church and state. On the other hand we have the pervasiveness of religion in American public and private life, accompanied and supported by its own constitutionally embodied legal norm—the free-exercise clause of the First Amendment.[2] How are we, then, to think about law, when the norm of separation seems in such tension with both the norm of free exercise and with actual practice?[3] Should the ideal of separation of church and state be abandoned as a hopeless dream? Is it the task of law and its enforcement machinery to attempt to change fundamentally the way people and public officials view the world? Is it even possible? Or can we find some workable accommodation between what the Constitution seems to require and what the world really looks like?

I thus want to look not only at the problems of religion and the law and religion and politics but also at religion as a case study of a larger issue: the *dispositional environment* of the law. The law does not write on a clean slate in the minds of those who are bound by the law and those who must enforce the law. Rather, people (whether subjects or enforcers) are likely to have certain predispositions about the subjects with which the law deals. What is the relationship between these predispositions and the way the law can or will be enforced? And what is the relationship between these predispositions and the likely effect of the law on actual behavior? In most areas, of course, dispositions themselves have been shaped by law. The relationship between law and public opinion seems symbiotic: neither can be said to be only the cause and none of the effect. Although this may also be the case with religion and with the issue of separation of church and state, religion, at least, is commonly taken to be largely pregovernmental and transgovernmental. That is, it is almost a defining characteristic of religion that its strictures and norms can be determined without reference to the law and without reference to the governmental organization of a particular political entity. With respect to questions of religion, therefore, the dispositional environment of the law is likely to be as little affected by that law as any subject can imaginably be. Religion and politics thus presents in quite pure form the relation between law and its dispositional environment. Looking at religion and the law from this perspective will enable us to think more clearly about the relation of law to human behavior.

I

Before turning specifically to the question of religion, I want to distinguish three different dispositional environments, corresponding to three different functions that law can be said to serve. Most often, law operates in an *enforcing* mode. In this mode the legal norm is widely accepted in the society, and the purpose of the legal norm and its enforcement is to prevent and sanction the occasional deviations from that norm. Laws against murder, child molestation, and keeping wild animals in residential areas all seem to fit this description. So too do some laws that involve no physical harm or danger, such as laws prohibiting the display of neon signs on private houses or laws requiring the wearing of clothes in public. Few people would be inclined to engage in the prohibited behavior even if there were no legal prohibition, so for most people the law is unnecessary. But the law serves to prevent deviance from this societally held value. Because in this mode there is substantial congruence between the law's mandate and what most people believe and would do anyway, there is likely to be little resistance to the law. Enforcing the law against those who deviate from the legal norm can be expected to be fully supported by the population, and we can predict that enforcement will be quite effective.[4]

At the opposite end of the spectrum we see law in its *forcing* mode. Here the legal norm is significantly at odds with prevailing public opinion. In some cases this may be because the law is ahead of public opinion, as for example with desegregation of the schools in the South at the time of *Brown* v. *Board of Education*.[5] At other times this may be because the law is behind changing trends with respect to public values, as might be said about laws against contraception in the 1960s.[6] Regardless of the sources of the divergence between law and prevailing behavior, if divergence exists the law is least likely to be effective. Prohibition is, of course, the most prominent example of this phenomenon and stands as a symbol of the difficulties of attempting to use law to guide public opinion and behavior in directions in which they are not otherwise inclined. This is not to say that law in its forcing mode is doomed to ineffectiveness. School desegregation demonstrates the extent to which, given a sufficient governmental investment in the enforcement process,[7] unpopular legal norms not only can be enforced but also can eventually shape public opinion itself.[8]

Between the poles of law as enforcing and as forcing we have the more prevalent mode of law as *reinforcing*. In this mode, public opinion and likely prelegal behavior are not nearly so in tune with the legal norm as they are in the murder and child molestation examples. Nor are they as inconsistent with the legal norm as in the examples of Prohibition and school desegregation. Rather, the legal norm reflects what society may believe in the abstract, but a combination of individual temptation and uncertainty about the correctness of the norm makes slippage likely. As a result, the legal norm is dispositive in determining the behavior of many people, but the norm itself is rather widely accepted. Most traffic laws fit this description, and so do a wide range of state and federal regulatory programs. The goal of safety at the workplace, for example, is hardly as unpopular in the abstract as Prohibition but hardly as self-enforcing as the societal strictures against indecent exposure. Occupational safety and health laws therefore can be seen as law in its reinforcing mode, playing an important controlling role with respect to the decisions of many people but still acceptable in the abstract to most of the population.

I do not intend my categories of forcing, enforcing, and reinforcing to be definitive, exhaustive, or mutually exclusive demarcations. Rather, I want them to be suggestive of a certain way of looking at the law, taking into account the relationship between what the law says on its face and how the law affects behavior. I want to focus not only on the carrots and sticks available from the legal side but also on the dispositional environment in which those carrots and sticks are used. This will affect our perception not only of whether to use carrots or sticks, and how many of each, but also of what the law itself ought to say.

II

For religious people, the commands of the deity take precedence over the commands of the secular state, at least in cases of conflict between the two. In light of this, much of our tradition relating to the free exercise of religion has tried to avoid putting people to this choice.[9] And even in areas in which the free-exercise clause of the First Amendment is noncontrolling, legislative action has frequently tried to prevent forcing people to do what their religious dictates say they should not. The best example of this is recognition of conscientious objection to military service[10] or to membership in a labor union.[11] But whether constitutionally or legislatively based, religion-premised and religion-tested exemptions from legal requirements that otherwise are universally applicable seem inspired by the recognition that law's forcing mode is least likely to be effective when the deviance between legal norm and individual opinion is inspired by an individual's religious beliefs.

The dispositional environment of the law is commonly taken to be significantly influenced by religion in areas such as abortion, obscenity, sodomy, euthanasia, Sunday closing, and state lotteries. More recently, religion has been taken by some to be relevant to issues such as the legitimacy of the Department of Education and a wide range of foreign policy questions. But I do not want to take on the entire range of issues in which religion influences public opinion and public behavior with respect to matters of legal purview. Rather, I want to focus specifically on the legal/constitutional norm of separation of church and state—the norm generally associated with the establishment clause of the First Amendment—and to explore the ways in which acceptance of or resistance to that norm should influence how we think about separation of church and state and about how courts should design the details of establishment-clause doctrine.

In considering the dispositional environment of a constitutional norm, we must first identify the identity of that environment. That is, to whom is the norm addressed? For until we locate the relevant population, we have no way of knowing what they think and what they do, and how their thinking and behavior are likely to be affected by the legal norm. But the primary addressee of a constitutional norm is different from that of a general regulatory statute; it is not the public at large but the state, or some legislative, executive, or judicial officials. These functionaries are all beholden to public opinion, and thus a constitutional norm indirectly acts on the population at large.

The norm of separation of church and state, in actual application, confronts a hostile dispositional environment.[12] As a result, in establishment-clause cases we are likely to see law in its forcing mode, rather than enforcing or reinforcing. Two alternative strategies follow from the identification of a forcing mode. One strategy takes as its guide the experience of Prohibition, as well as the dictum of (surprisingly) Justice Douglas that "we are a religious people whose institutions presuppose a Supreme Being."[13] Thus, this first strategy treats separation of church and state as a norm in tension with unchangeable human beliefs and practices and focuses on ways of incorporating the inevitable into legal doctrine. By contrast, the alternative strategy takes not Prohibition but school desegregation as its inspiring legal/political event and looks at the possibility that law in its forcing mode can have a significant impact, even in a hostile dispositional environment. This strategy does not try to conform the legal norm to preexisting dispositions but rather concentrates on those aspects of the enforcement machinery that may make it possible for legal norms to play a significant role in constructing a behavioral reality that may not at present exist.

III

Since in most instances the application of the norm confronts a hostile dispositional environment, there is likely to be some slippage between the behavior legally desired and the behavior actually produced. But in order to make the statement that there will be resistance to the application of the norm, we must distinguish between the abstract articulation of a legal value and the instances of its contemporary application.

Many values sound quite acceptable to most people when articulated as "majestic generalities" but they seem much less acceptable when presented as specific resolutions of specific issues. This is certainly true with freedom of speech and criminal procedure, and it seems true of freedom of religion as well. There is little doubt that most Americans today would agree that the separation of church and state is a good thing. Nor do I have reason to question whether Americans would support the idea that there should be no official, established state church in the United States.[14] But the questions that now concern us in thinking about the establishment clause are not abstract questions like these. Instead, they are the questions that have frequently been before the courts in the last thirty years. Should there be organized prayer in the public schools?[15] Should schools be permitted to display the Ten Commandments on school property?[16] Should prayers be permitted in legislatures when led by a chaplain paid by the state?[17] Should Christmas displays including religious symbols be permitted in a public park?[18] Do Sunday closing laws violate the Constitution?[19] Does state assistance to private schools, including private parochial schools, involve unconstitutionally excessive state aid of religion?[20] Should church property be exempt from property taxes?[21]

Let us think now about how these issues are perceived by the public, and also about how they are perceived by those state and local officials whose actions are questioned in cases like these. I want to offer several hypotheses, all of them empirical in nature, none of them supported by empirical evidence here, yet all of them to me intuitively sound. First, if with respect to all of these issues the Supreme Court had decided consistently in favor of the state practice and thus consistently against the establishment-clause challenge, there would have been no pervasive public outcry, no call for a constitutional amendment, and no congressional stirrings about limitations on the Supreme Court's jurisdiction.[22] Second, in many instances in which the courts have decided in favor of the establishment-clause claim and against state practices, there has been a consistent pattern of resistance and even disobedience of the constitutional decisions by state officials. School prayer is the most obvious example, although the phenomenon of disobedience is plainly concentrated in smaller localities.[23] Third, in many other instances in which courts have decided in favor of establishment-clause claims and against state practices, state legislative and executive officials frequently and persistently have attempted to come up with schemes that would be in literal compliance with court rulings but would allow the state in effect to continue the questionable practice.[24] This has happened in the school prayer area and also quite frequently with respect to public financing of parochial school education. Fourth, public or official acceptance of court decisions upholding establishment-clause claims in the specified areas has not significantly increased in the last twenty-five years. If anything, it has decreased.

If these empirical hypotheses are correct, and I have no reason to believe that they are not, then it becomes clear that in specific cases the enforcement of establishment-clause norms is difficult. The relevant mode is that of forcing not only unwilling citizens but also unwilling officials. Moreover, the body most directly responsible for the decisions, the Supreme Court, is the body least able to enforce its norms.[25] While this phenomenon is not unique to the establishment clause, it does seem particularly striking here, and it does distinguish establishment-clause issues from many law enforcement problems outside the realm of constitutional litigation.

The forcing mode is especially difficult when the recalcitrant addressees of the legal norms are not speakeasy operators and bootleggers but elected and appointed public officials. Moreover, if those who object to the constitutional norms perceive their objections as divinely inspired, what hope is there of dissipating those objections? What, then, does this characterization of the dispositional environment have to say about the present and future state of the relevant constitutional norms? Should the law back off? Should it instead continue to swim upstream against contrary and seemingly unmalleable public and official opinion? Or is some accommodation possible?

IV

The first strategy for dealing with law in its forcing mode is what might be called a strategy of submission. Its premise is inevitability, and its goal is the avoidance of the tension that puts law into the forcing mode in the first instance. It is thus a strategy that tries to make law conform to the broad outlines of preexisting behavior and is content, therefore, with relatively small, incremental effects on behavior. In exchange for relinquishing the ambitious goal of effecting significant changes in behavior, it gains a high degree of compliance with its modest aspirations. It thus may bring two advantages. One is the possibility that more may be done if less is tried. In the face of clear resistance, a more ambitious agenda may produce no change in behavior whatsoever. But a less ambitious agenda may be able to marshal its enforcement apparatus, as well as appeal more successfully to public opinion and thus actually accomplish more. A strategy of submission also offers advantages to the legal system generally, for that system suffers when it is—and is perceived to be—ineffective. The lack of acceptance of law in one substantive area is likely to have spillover effects throughout law. Thus it can be argued in favor of the strategy of submission that it may sacrifice particular goals, but it does so in the service of the even larger goal of maintaining the integrity of the legal system generally or, here, the constitutional system in particular.

Take, for example, the question of school prayer. It is commonly assumed that since 1963, a significant amount of teacher-sponsored or at least teacher-approved prayer has taken place in the public schools. One of the significant issues surrounding both past and potential "moment of silence" cases brought before the Supreme Court[26] is the question of what will actually take place in the classroom if the moment-of-silence provision is upheld. One argument made by challengers of such laws is that this will make it easier for teachers to encourage prayer despite the appearance of the law to the contrary.

Under the strategy of submission, the question is not whether teachers will use a moment of silence to sneak prayer into the classrooms, for the presupposition is that prayer is most likely already sneaking into the classrooms and in many cases not even sneakily. If this presupposition is correct, then why put courts in a position of having their mandates unenforced? Moreover, relying solely on unenforced mandates takes the courts out of any monitoring role at all. If the courts say that no prayer of any kind can take place, they cannot then be in a position of looking realistically at the circumstances in which prayer is in fact taking place.[27] Acknowledging that prayer will inevitably take place in the schools, however, allows the courts to play a more active role with a less ambitious agenda. The moment of silence, for example, might succeed in confining school prayer within limits acceptable to a wide range of the population, in a way that current practices may not. The analogy with Prohibition again comes to mind. Prohibition effectively disables the law from controlling the price and quality of alcoholic beverages. The end result is that people who are going to drink regardless of whether or not it is illegal will wind up paying high prices for potentially dangerous substances. But if Prohibition is relinquished in favor of milder controls, then price and quality can be more effectively monitored.

A similar analysis might be applied to the crèche cases.[28] If we assume that public officials inevitably will feel compelled to engage in some public sponsorship of major religious symbols and holidays, then it is perhaps appropriate to bring this activity into the open, with some degree of explicit permission, rather than engaging in an ineffectual and counterproductive total prohibition. And we might also view school financing cases in the same way. If some support is inevitable, or if there is no likelihood that the population will ever internalize the norms of nonsupport embodied in *Lemon* v. *Kurtzman*,[29] then maybe law, having tried its best, should attempt to adapt its strictures to prevailing societal norms, rather than the other way around.

The strategy of submission can be seen as an attempt to avoid the phenomenon of ineffectual constitutional norms. But it can be seen in another light as well. Where conflicting values are at work, the wise course may be not to choose one or another. And it may not even endeavor to come up with some balancing approach that (usually futilely) tries to accommodate all of the relevant interests. Perhaps in some areas religion will be kept strictly away from any aspect of government and in other areas the inevitable intertwining of the two will be acknowledged. We resolve the conflict not by balancing, and not by quixotically choosing one or another for exclusive concern, but by choosing both, each with an area in which it can flourish and an area from which it is prohibited.[30]

V

Opposed to a strategy of submission is what can be called a *strategy of compulsion*. Here the inevitability of disobedience and the futility of trying to change public or legislative or executive views are taken not as causes of resignation but as challenges. As the school desegregation experience may teach us, a frequently successful response to the phenomenon of the forcing mode is an increase in enforcement resources and commitment. Especially where the legal norm can be historically and linguistically traced to the Constitution, the official and symbolic authority of that document can provide the impetus to overcome, at least partially, substantial resistance. However, this requires a commitment from more than just the judicial system. Possibly one of the most important constitutional decisions in American history was made not by the Supreme Court but by President Eisenhower with reference to Little Rock.[31] By agreeing to commit the federal military power to enforcing a decision with which he disagreed, Eisenhower established more than any court could have the authority of both the Constitution and the Supreme Court's interpretation of it. Should the political branches of state and federal governments take the same view with respect to Supreme Court decisions regarding separation of church and state, then we might see a parallel amount of success despite a hostile dispositional environment.

One approach evolving out of a strategy of compulsion is to redouble the law's efforts to have its mandates enforced, but there is another that is probably more significant. For it is not necessarily the case that underenforced legal norms serve no purpose. This may be especially true with respect to constitutional norms. The norm stands as a symbol that a given principle, without exception, is centrally important in this society. Some constitutional norms may serve a function not dissimilar to that served by, say, Santa Claus. Santa Claus, to the best of my knowledge, does not exist as a fat old man who makes toys at the North Pole and delivers them in a sleigh every Christmas. But the unreality of the characterization does not detract from the importance of Santa Claus as symbol, and I would not eliminate Santa Claus as symbol even though I have little hope that he will come down my chimney next December. Legal norms, even if in some respects unrealistic and unenforceable, likewise may serve important symbolic purposes.

From this perspective, the norms embodied in the establishment clause should not be weakened in the face of significant resistance. If greater enforcement is not possible, then perhaps it is even more necessary for the judiciary and other public officials to magnify the strength of the establishment clause as symbol. This would include, therefore, close attention to violations that many might perceive as trivial. It is unlikely that courts are going to strike down "In God We Trust" on our coins as an unconstitutional violation of the establishment clause,[32] enjoin bailiffs from announcing "God Save the United States of America and this Honorable Court," or prohibit astronauts from praying while in their federally sponsored space capsule.[33] But there may be many other cases, such as the Ten Commandments case[34] or the crèche cases, that in some sense are trivial but in another sense are symbolically important. For unlike many of the school financing issues, the conjunction of church and state here is highly and recurrently visible, and the simplicity of the factual setting may give court decisions especial prominence. And if we are concerned with the establishment clause as symbol, the lack of enforceability of that symbol may be little cause for retrenchment.

This symbolic approach and the strategy of compulsion may have particular merit in the context of individual rights under the Constitution. Certain of these individual rights, including many involving freedom of speech, freedom of religion, and criminal procedure, are in the document for protective purposes. They protect individuals from government; they protect minorities, broadly defined, from majorities; and they protect us from ourselves. They entrench certain long-term values in order to protect them from being threatened by short-term exigencies, some of which may be very important and very real. Because there is such a temptation for people as well as governments to mortgage the future for present advantage, it becomes necessary, or at least has been seen as necessary, to exclude certain matters from this phenomenon. Some individual rights in the Constitution may be akin to removing all of the cigarettes from the house if you are trying to quit smoking. In contemplative times one removes the temptations that might seem compelling in the future.

If we look at the norms of separation of church and state in this way, then we can see that these norms are designed to serve strikingly different purposes from the more conventional regulatory norms of the law. They are not, at least exclusively, designed to change views or to change behavior. Moreover, they are inherently and structurally countermajoritarian. If their enforcement creates tension, hostility, and therefore resistance, and if their continued enforcement does little to secure acceptance of the underlying value, we should not be disappointed. The phenomenon we anticipated all along is in fact occurring, and the very reasons for having the establishment clause in the first instance are being realized. To abandon a strategy of compulsion in favor of a strategy of submission, it can be argued, is ultimately to allow the decision to be made by the majority of the people. This, of course, makes perfect sense with the normal regulatory standards of the law. But the norms of the establishment clause are there as a protection against the majority, and it seems odd to permit that majority, the group we wanted to control in the first place, to determine the extent of that protection.[35]

VI

I have tried to sketch broadly the main lines of argument that would support either a strategy of submission (to state and local governments and to current majorities) or a strategy of compulsion (of state and local governments and of current majorities). I have not tried to argue, at least at great length, why one or the other strategy should be adopted. Nor have I tried to explore ways in which some elements of both strategies might be combined into an optimal solution to the problems raised. At this point, suggesting a framework for discussion seems more important than taking strong ultimate positions on the issues. But let me conclude by suggesting that one's view about these issues may parallel one's view about dealing with the problems of inevitability, hostility, and resistance in the context of the establishment clause.

The Constitution of the United States contains no explicit or even implicit exceptions for war, national defense, or other national emergency. Yet most students of individual rights know full well that in times of war or other periods of intense national engagement, individual rights against government and against majorities are likely to be less stringently protected. We have witnessed this phenomenon with respect to the free-speech cases of the First World War,[36] the Japanese internment cases in the Second World War,[37] and many of the cases of the McCarthy era.[38] Many students of the Constitution believe that, however much we may criticize after the fact, the judiciary can never be firmly antimajoritarian or firmly antigovernment or firmly antimilitary in times of war and other national emergencies, real or perceived. If that is the case, then should not the Constitution contain an explicit exception or safety valve for these periods? This question has arisen recently with respect to various new constitutions and charters for the protection of individual rights. On the one hand it can be argued that, since exceptions will be found in any event, an explicit exceptions clause preserves the fidelity of the rule of law and prevents the distortion of text, precedent, and doctrine that comes when exceptions must be found against the background of exceptionless principles. On the other hand it is argued that even if exceptions will be found, it is better not to invite them, for inviting them by an explicit exceptions clause in the end will result in more incursions on constitutional principle than would be the case if those incursions, however inevitable, were treated as technically illegitimate. How one comes out on this question, it seems to me, is likely to be strongly suggestive of how one feels about establishment-clause doctrine. Even those who believe strongly in Jefferson's well-worn metaphor of the "wall of separation" must admit that that wall has, and always will have, cracks in it. The question now before us is whether we will accept the existence of those cracks, or whether we will try to build a lower wall with fewer cracks.

Notes

1. "Congress shall make no law respecting an establishment of religion," U.S. Const., Amend. 1. It is by now well accepted that the establishment clause is, by virtue of incorporation within the concept of liberty in the Fourteenth Amendment, a restriction on the states as well as on the federal government. *Everson* v. *Board of Education*, 390 U.S. 1 (1947); see also *Abington School District* v. *Schempp*, 374 U.S. 203 (1963) (Brennan, J., concurring).

2. ". . . , or prohibiting the free exercise thereof," U.S. Const., Amend. 1.

3. Although the details of First Amendment doctrine with respect to freedom of religion are not my agenda here, the tension between the two constitutional clauses has been a recurrent problem for the courts. See *Widmar* v. *Vincent*, 454 U.S. 263 (1981); *Sherbert* v. *Verner*, 374 U.S. 398 (1963) (Stewart, J., concurring).

4. I do not intend to be taken as suggesting a perfect correlation between supportive public opinion and effective enforcement. Many other variables are relevant, some of which in some circumstances might detract from the effectiveness of enforce-

ment of widely respected laws. But it does seem likely that for many factors public
support is closely related to increasing enforcement effectiveness. For example,
public acceptance will help to increase the resources available for governmental
enforcement of the laws at issue, will likely correlate with judges, juries, and
police officers sympathetic with the enforcement goals, and will increase the availability of informal social sanctions to reinforce the formal sanctions of the law.

5. 347 U.S. 483 (1954).

6. See *Griswold v. Connecticut*, 381 U.S. 479 (1965). One of the more interesting
features of the background of *Griswold* was the difficulty that Griswold and Dr.
Buxton had in getting themselves prosecuted in order to test the constitutionality
of the statute prohibiting the distribution of contraceptives.

7. Also relevant is the authoritative pedigree of the source of the unpopular norm.
The better the pedigree—that is, the more the source of the norm has its own
capital of respect and authority independent of the particular decision—the more
likely it is that an unpopular norm will be respected. Thus it may make a difference, even apart from straight enforcement considerations, whether a norm ema-
nates from the Supreme Court, a legislature, the executive, or a bureaucrat. But
which of these sources will have greater or lesser authoritative pedigrees will vary
considerably with time, place, and decisional context.

8. This phenomenon of law being a leader of public opinion is, of course, not restricted to judicial decisions. In many areas, such as environmental law and con-
sumer protection, the wishes of a vocal and powerful minority are embodied into
law. At that point the symbolic force of law as well as the sanctions behind it serves
to propagate the view that the opinion now embodied in the law is correct. In
these cases law is part of the process by which public opinion changes, and it is an
oversimplification to say that law necessarily follows public opinion. Sometimes it
helps to lead it. This perspective of law as a shaper of rather than reactor to public
opinion is a matter of considerable contemporary scholarly interest.

9. See e.g., *Wisconsin v. Yoder*, 406 U.S. 205 (1972); *Sherbert v. Verner*, 374 U.S. 398
(1963); *Thomas v. Indiana Review Board of Employment Security*, 450 U.S. 707
(1981). To similar effect are the cases that combine free speech and free exercise
elements, such as *West Virginia Board of Education v. Barnette*, 319 U.S. 624 (1943),
and *Wooley v. Maynard*, 430 U.S. 705 (1977). But there is also the opposing legal/
political tradition, one that requires people living in a secular state to submit to
neutral and secular controls even if doing so would offend their own religious
beliefs. See, e.g., *Reynolds v. United States*, 98 U.S. 145 (1878) (polygamy); *Jacob-
son v. Massachusetts*, 197 U.S. 111 (1905) (vaccination); *Prince v. Massachusetts*,
321 U.S. 158 (1944) (child labor); *Bob Jones University v. United States*, 461 U.S.
574 (1983) (racial discrimination).

10. See *United States v. Seeger*, 380 U.S. 163 (1965); *Gillette v. United States*, 401 U.S.
437 (1971).

11. 29 U.S.C. sec. 169 (Supp. 1984).

12. "The subject seems peculiarly well calculated to generate resistance and backlash

and peculiarly ill calculated to enlist adequate countervailing support. Congressmen feel that defending prayer is like defending motherhood: it wins them some votes and costs them almost none." Robert McCloskey, "Principles, Powers, and Values: The Establishment Clause and the Supreme Court," *Religion and Public Organization* 3(1964):28.

13. *Zorach v. Clauson,* 343 U.S. 306 (1952).

14. There is no doubt that preventing the establishment of an official state church was one of the original purposes of the establishment clause. There is considerable historical controversy, however, about whether it was the only purpose. See generally Philip Kurland, *Religion and the Law* (Chicago: University of Chicago Press, 1962); Frederick Schauer, "An Essay on Constitutional Language," *UCLA Law Review* 29 (1982):797–832.

15. *Abington School District v. Schempp,* 374 U.S. 203 (1963); *Engel v. Vitale,* 370 U.S. 421 (1962).

16. *Stone v. Graham,* 449 U.S. 39 (1980).

17. *Marsh v. Chambers,* 463 U.S. 624 (1983).

18. *Lynch v. Donnelly,* 104 S. Ct. 1355 (1984).

19. *McGowan v. Maryland,* 366 U.S. 420 (1961).

20. *Mueller v. Allen,* 103 S. Ct. 3062 (1983); *Committee for Public Education & Religious Liberty v. Regan,* 100 S. Ct. 840 (1980); *Lemon v. Kurtzman,* 403 U.S. 602 (1971).

21. *Walz v. Tax Commissioner,* 397 U.S. 664 (1970).

22. On actions to curb the Supreme Court's jurisdiction in school prayer (and other) cases, see Lawrence Sager, "Foreword: Constitutional Limitations on Congress' Authority to Regulate the Jurisdiction of the Federal Courts," *Harvard Law Review* 95 (1981): 17–90. On the proposed constitutional amendment dealing with school prayer, see *Congressional Quarterly Weekly Report* 42 (March 24, 1984):643–44.

23. See Dolbeare & Hammond, *The School Prayer Decisions: From Court Policy to Local Practice* (1971); Katz, *Patterns of Compliance with the Schempp Decision,* 14 J. Public L. 396 (1965); Beaney & Beiser, *Prayer and Politics: The Impact of Engel and Schempp on the Political Process,* 13 J. Public L. 475 (1964).

24. See *Wallace v. Jaffree,* 472 U.S. 38 (1985).

25. See generally Alexander Bickel, *The Least Dangerous Branch* (Indianapolis: Bobbs-Merrill Co., 1962).

26. *Wallace v. Jaffree,* 472 U.S. 38 (1985); *May v. Cooperman,* 780 F.2d 240 (3rd Cir. 1985).

27. This kind of looking, however, may involve a separate problem under contemporary establishment clause doctrine, the problem of entanglement. See *Lemon v. Kurtzman,* 403 U.S. 602 (1971); *Larkin v. Grendel's Den, Inc.,* 454 U.S. 116 (1982).

28. *Lynch* v. *Donnelly,* 104 S. Ct. 1355 (1984); *Board of Trustees of the Village of Scars-dale* v. *McCreary,* affirming decision below by an equally divided Court: 739 F.2d 716 (2d Cir. 1984).

29. 403 U.S. 602 (1971).

30. The idea expressed in the text is an adaptation to the problem of freedom of religion of the perspective on freedom of speech and freedom of the press offered by my colleague Lee Bollinger. See Bollinger, "Freedom of the Press and Public Access: Toward a Theory of Partial Regulation of the Mass Media," *Michigan Law Review* 75 (1976):1–44.

31. The relevant Supreme Court opinion is *Cooper* v. *Aaron,* 358 U.S. 1 (1958).

32. *Aronow* v. *United States,* 432 F.2d 242 (9th Cir. 1970).

33. *O'Hair* v. *Payne,* 432 F.2d 66 (5th Cir. 1970), cert. denied, 401 U.S. 955 (1971).

34. *Stone* v. *Graham,* 449 U.S. 39 (1980).

35. On the anomalous nature of allowing a majority to determine the scope and strength of rights against that majority, see Ronald Dworkin, *Taking Rights Seriously* (Cambridge: Harvard University Press, 1977).

36. *Schenck* v. *United States,* 249 U.S. 47 (1919); *Frohwerk* v. *United States,* 249 U.S. 204 (1919); *Debs* v. *United States,* 249 U.S. 211 (1919); *Abrams* v. *United States,* 250 U.S. 616 (1919).

37. *Korematsu* v. *United States,* 323 U.S. 214 (1944); *Hirabayashi* v. *United States,* 320 U.S. 81 (1943).

38. *Dennis* v. *United States,* 341 U.S. 494 (1951); *Adler* v. *Board of Education,* 342 U.S. 485 (1952).

Religion and Politics in the United States in the Next Fifteen Years

ROBERT F. DRINAN, S.J.

Is the traditional symbiosis that has always existed between religion and government in America eroding? Are churches seeking too vigorously to change some basic governmental policies? What will the influence of the churches be like in the year 2000? Those are just a few of the questions that come to mind as one reflects upon the fact that the United States Supreme Court has dealt with an unprecedented number of major church-state cases in recent years. One can wonder nonetheless whether those decisions will change in any significant way the church-state scene as it has evolved over the past forty years.

Church-state relations in America have been remarkably stable and static since 1947, when the Supreme Court for the first time transmitted the establishment clause of the First Amendment to the states by way of the Fourteenth Amendment and in so doing ruled, five to four, that free bus rides constituted the maximum in financial aid that could be given to children in Catholic schools. The relationship between government and religion on another front has been similarly stable since the Supreme Court in 1952 held that released-time religious education could be held off the school premises but not on school property.

Indeed in retrospect the controversies over aid to church-related schools and about religion in the public schools seem now to be less turbulent than they appeared at the time they arose. In fact, it is now clear that over the past two generations there has been a remarkably firm consensus with respect to the traditional arrangement of church and state—no aid to church-related schools and no sectarian religion in the public schools. The country, in other words, has more or less agreed with the Supreme Court's repeated insistence that no substantial aid go to religiously affiliated schools and that no sectarian practices be introduced into the public school.

The forthcoming eight decisions of the Supreme Court may alter that arrangement somewhat if the Court sustains the law allowing a moment of silence in twenty-two states and eases the restrictions on shared-time or dual-enrollment arrangements for church-related schools. But even if the Court sharply deviates from the formula by which it has integrated the establishment and the free exercise clauses, it is not clear that the arrangements legally mandated for four decades will change very much. And even if prayer is returned to the public school and some aid is granted to church-related schools, the basic orientation and place of the public and private schools may not be radically altered.

On the other hand there are some signs that the forces that produced the present consensus may be changing. That change could be brought about by the emergence of two new major players—the fundamentalists and the Catholics—both of whom are aggressively advancing their positions in the forum of public opinion. The sound and fury of these groups is escalating. It is not clear that either group has yet altered the consensus developed and agreed to by mainline Protestants, the Jewish community, liberal groups, and humanists; but the two new religious groups acting sometimes alone and sometimes together may well be in a position to alter the church-state picture in America. It might be helpful, therefore, to try to analyze the forces that are operating in both groups.

A remarkable transformation continues to occur in the self-image and the aspirations of the Catholic community in America. Now with 52 million adherents, 300 bishops, 50,000 priests, and 120,000 nuns, the Catholic church is vibrant with a feeling of maturing. The sense of being a minority in a pan-Protestant nation has sharply diminished. Catholics continue to be pleased and proud of their school system, which educates some 3 million children. They have a special affection for the 200 Catholic colleges—even for those institutions whose reputations are at best regional or local. And they want to be known and heard in an America where, more than at any time in the past, they feel they belong and matter.

Catholics who have engaged in ecumenical conversations with Protestants have become familiar with Protestant thought and organization in America, but such familiarity is not common among Catholics. The theological and social distances between Catholics and Protestants are still significant. But these distances may be eroding more rapidly than is perceived at this time. One has to wonder what might happen to traditional church-state patterns if mainline Protestants and Catholics were to come into fundamental agreement on major issues of public morality. As of now, significant and deep differences exist between the official Protestant and Catholic positions on the availability of state aid for church-related schools and on the wisdom of recriminalizing abortion. But there is a deepening feeling among many Christians that the onslaught of secularism in American life requires all religious bodies to speak and act together to prevent the erosion of those fundamental moral values on which America's very existence depends. Positions taken by the National Council of Churches (NCC), which represents most mainline Protestant bodies, and the positions set forth by the U.S. Catholic Conference (USCC) have been very similar on the war in Vietnam, the enactment and enforcement of civil rights laws, and issues related to poverty and hunger in America. On other issues there is also a parallelism, as for example on the desirability of a new immigration law, the treatment of refugees, the desirability of a nonmilitary policy for Central America, and the level of United States foreign aid.

Perhaps the central issue in church-state relations in the next fifteen years is the capacity of the mainline Protestant churches allied with the official Catholic church to influence public morality in foreign policy in the United States. If these two powerful forces would form a working alliance on several issues, they might well be in a position to have a very significant impact on how the United States government thinks and acts. Although the NCC and the USCC hold many positions in common, there does not yet appear to be a conscious attempt to pool their common resources and influence on behalf of a common objective. There may be too many historical and psychological barriers between the NCC and the USCC to permit open and public collaboration even on those issues on which their positions are virtually identical.

The issue of nuclear war may possibly be the question that could bring together the moral and organizational power of the mainline Protestants and America's Catholics. After the Catholic bishops issued their well-received and carefully nuanced pastoral on nuclear warfare in

1983, the NCC, meeting in solemn assembly in San Francisco, explicitly endorsed the results and the reasoning of the Catholic bishops' pastoral. That endorsement, totally unprecedented in the annals of Catholic-Protestant relations in this country, has the most significant implications. What would happen if the total organizational power of the NCC combined with the energies of the Catholics in America? No one can predict since it has never happened before, at least in the dramatic manner in which the USCC's conclusions on nuclear war have been accepted and endorsed by the NCC. This agreement between the USCC and the NCC is all the more remarkable when it is realized that the bishops' pastoral rejects some of the fundamental major premises of United States foreign policy over the past thirty years. The pastoral letter affirms Vatican II in condemning the use of nuclear weapons for any purpose whatsoever while allowing their continued possession for the purpose of deterrence only on the condition that a plan is being developed to phase them out. The pastoral also urges the United States to withdraw from its policy of relying on the first use of nuclear weapons and to abandon plans to build the MX. The pastoral, in other words, is a rejection of several of the basic assumptions behind the strategic policies of the United States since the Eisenhower administration. To have the mainline Protestants and the Catholic community agree on this approach is, of course, extraordinarily significant.

Most church-state issues seem unimportant compared to the forthcoming potential confrontation of the major churches in America with the stated policies of the government on the contemplated use of massive nuclear forces to contain Communism. The churches have stated in essence that the government has adopted and followed principles of massive retaliation or the threat of force, which are incompatible with basic Christian morality. Will the churches join ranks in refining and explaining their condemnation of nuclear weapons? This condemnation, set forth in a less developed way in Vatican II in 1965, has now become the most important challenge by the churches of America to the government of the United States in the whole history of the nation, with the possible exception of the nineteenth-century church-related movement to abolish slavery.

Father Richard McCormick, S.J., a noted moral theologian, described well the forthcoming challenge when he wrote in the March 1982 issue of *Theological Studies* that the "religious leadership in the

United States, especially Catholic, is on a collision course with the U.S. government. That just may be the best thing to happen to both in a long time."

Some of the potential political implications of the church-inspired opposition to nuclear war were dramatized by the opposition of the USCC to the MX as announced on the first page of the *New York Times* on March 16, 1985. It remains to be seen whether the NCC will follow suit or whether the USCC, with or without the NCC, can influence the outcome of a series of votes predictably close in both houses of Congress. But regardless of the ultimate result, it is clear that a new phase of church-state confrontation has arrived when the official Catholic body, representing 23 percent of the nation's citizens, sends to every member of Congress a statement opposing one of the central postulates of the military strategy of the Reagan administration.

The potential consequences of a newly energized and to some extent politicized Catholic hierarchy may take some time to unfold. It is possible that many Catholics or millions of others will openly or quietly disagree with the bishops' condemnation of nuclear deterrence and the MX. These individuals may go along with the unprecedented and massive military buildup being implemented by the Reagan administration. If this occurs, one of the causes will be the rise beginning in 1980 of the political phenomenon of religious fundamentalists and especially the birth of the Moral Majority. It is difficult if not impossible to evaluate the impact of this group on the elections of 1980 and 1984. The claims of the religious right as to their political influence, and particularly the claims of the Reverend Jerry Falwell, president of the Moral Majority, have been exaggerated. Religious fundamentalists have always existed and have been a conservative and reactionary political force. They might have voted the same way in 1980 and 1984 even if their leaders had not become politicized. But it does seem nonetheless that the religious right is a newly organized moral and political force and that some of its main thrusts are diametrically opposed to some of the points of agreement between the NCC and the USCC.

What impact on traditional church-state relations will the leaders of the religious right have in the next fifteen years? These leaders may obtain some form of tuition tax credits for the parents of students in evangelical church-sponsored schools, whose number is escalating. They may persuade the Congress and the country to pass an amendment to the Constitution permitting prayer to be recited in public schools. And they may have some success in cutting back on the constitutional right of women to terminate a pregnancy.

More importantly, however, can the religious right win over millions of Christians and nonbelievers to their viewpoint that the nation must increase its military strength against the Communists, who in the rhetoric of the religious right are sometimes called the Antichrist? As of now, spokespersons for the religious fundamentalists have not been able to persuade the American people that the United States should defeat the alleged Communists in Central America by military might; Americans are opposed to such a course by a vote of almost four to one. But the contention of the religious right that the United States must be armed in a holy war against Marxism in the Soviet Union and around the world has an appeal in the United States to the military, to the 28 million veterans, to many conservative forces, and to those groups in the NCC-USCC community who have always feared the Communist presence as a menace to Christianity.

The deepest struggle between government and religion that is now going on in America involves the attempts to win the minds and hearts of Americans of the Protestant-Catholic antinuclear alliance and the pro-God and pro-America religious right. If the Protestant-Catholic alliance holds and grows, there could be a dramatic halt and even a reversal in the nation's armaments, which now number 30,000 nuclear weapons with three more added every day—1,300 each year. If, on the other hand, the religious right is able to form a coalition of evangelical fundamentalists and doctrinaire anti-Communists, the nation could continue to add weapons and anti-Communist policies of all kinds.

When present and future church-state struggles are viewed in this light, the presence or absence of prayer in the public school seems like a trivial and inconsequential issue. But the prayer question—so all-consuming to some adherents of the religious right—is a test of how people view the Republic. Is it a godly nation consecrated to the Kingdom of the Lord? Is the public school required or mandated to instill piety along with patriotism?

The insistence that the government embrace and endorse religion is one of the basic tenets of the religious right. Spokespersons for the fundamentalists may deny that they want the government to favor religion openly, but they always denounce the ungodly state, and in secular humanism they find the very special enemy of all things good.

The Reverend Jerry Falwell has pleaded vigorously for the return of prayers to the schools. But he also declared to the Conservative Rabbinical Assembly of America in March 1985 that "we are not a Christian nation. We don't want a state church. This is a pluralistic society." Falwell also stated that "schools should be neutral."[1] That profession, however, does not cancel out all of the countless declarations by advocates of the new religious right that the United States is a Christian nation, that political candidates who are not born-again Christians are amoral, and that some elections are apocalyptic struggles between Christ and the Antichrist.

By clear implication Protestants of the religious right must be prepared to hold that American domestic and foreign policy should carry out the teaching of the Christian churches in America. And again by clear implication the defenders of the fundamentalists' new right have to claim that they and not the NCC represent authentic Christianity at this time. The Falwells of the last several years make it clear that in their judgment the NCC has been too liberal and permissive, too soft on Communism, and totally wrong in its attitudes toward abortion, prayer in the public schools, the Equal Rights Amendment, and tuition tax credits for religiously affiliated schools. The indictment of the NCC carries over to its attitudes toward the World Council of Churches (WCC) and the alleged laxity of the WCC toward the alleged spread of Communism into the Third World. In short, the religious right is opposed on essential issues to the attitudes and programs of the NCC.

The religious right feels more at ease with some American Catholics. Fundamentalists agree with the request of the Catholic bishops for tax relief for church-related schools and enthusiastically applaud the bishops' appeal for a constitutional amendment to outlaw abortion. But the fundamentalists have been unable or unwilling to make common cause with Catholic forces in their appeal for a government that does more rather than less for the poor and the minorities. Nor has the religious right concurred with the Catholic bishops in their insistent call for a halt to military aid to the government in El Salvador and to the contras that want to topple the Sandinistas.

It is unclear whether the affinities of the religious right and the official Catholic position on abortion and state aid to church-related schools will help to bring about a political bloc that could be decisive in some elections. Clearly the Catholic bishops have done their best to prevent such a development. In early 1984 the bishops reiterated their traditional message that Catholics should vote on a broad variety of issues and not on one issue alone. The bishops named fourteen issues, one of which was, of course, abortion. It is noteworthy that at their annual meeting in November 1984 after the election, the bishops reiterated their position and in effect rebuked unnamed bishops who failed to follow the directives of the hierarchy and stressed the position of certain candidates on abortion as the central issue in the election.

By 1985, then, a relatively new constellation of factors and actors was operating in the church-state area in America. If election results are a reliable guide, it appears that the Jewish community was clearly with the liberal elements in the NCC-USCC groups, since about 70 percent of Jewish voters cast their ballot for Walter Mondale.

Religious groups in America probably reflect opinions that cover the full spectrum of opinions in the United States. But the far left and the far right within the churches seem to have an influence disproportionate to their numbers. Perhaps it has always been so, but the struggle to fashion the basic tenets of America's public morality seems at the present time to be a contest beetween the left liberal policies of the NCC and the USCC and the right conservative positions of the Moral Majority and the fundamentalists. A clear-cut victory for either side on most issues is not likely. But in the next fifteen years the United States and the world will be faced with such immense moral problems that the churches cannot be silent, and in the end one faction within the churches will be able to claim more victories for its positions than any other religious group. The power struggle between the religious left and the religious right, therefore, has to be resolved at least on some issues. It may take decades or generations to play out, but in the year 2000 some decisions, reached by action or inaction, will have been reached.

The churches may continue to focus on issues resolved by the Supreme Court in June 1985. These issues include the constitutionality of crèches on public property, the moment of silence in the public school, and tax-supported teachers giving supplementary education in church-related schools. The churches almost certainly will focus their attention on the role of religious bodies regarding political campaigns and the propriety of politically oriented statements by tax-exempt religious groups. The churches and commentators on the churches will describe these issues as central, crucial, and critical. But any adequate assessment of what inevitably is going to happen in the next fifteen years has to result in the conclusion that most of these issues are inconsequential, even trivial, when compared to the morally compelling agonies that will develop in the global village before the year 2000. If the churches of America do not set aside or rise above their understandable involvement in traditional church-state disputes and try to help all of humanity, historians in the year 2000 and beyond will conclude that the churches in the generation from 1980 to 2000 spent their energies on problems of little ultimate consequence while the world cried out for guidance and help from all of the developed nations and particularly from the United States.

Every Christian has to be shocked and scandalized at the injustices that exist and that are increasing in the Third World. Consider some of the basic developments.

1. In the next fifteen years the population of the world will increase by 2 billion human beings. The number of persons on the planet will grow from 4.2 billion to 6.2 billion. Nothing can deter this rise in population, the sharpest in any period of history. It is clear that little planning of any kind is being done for the 140 million new men and women who join mankind each year. If a surge of population comparable to this were anticipated within the United States, the churches and hopefully the government would be deeply involved in marshaling resources for the construction of schools, houses, and health facilities. No Christian can excuse Christian bodies in the United States from being unconcerned with fellow human beings because they are suffering 6,000 miles away in Africa or Asia rather than in Boston or Berkeley. The Gospel mandates that those who have superfluous goods are required to share them with those who are homeless and hungry anywhere in the world. The churches have generally been supportive over the past generation of UNICEF, the World Health Organization (WHO), the Food and Agriculture Organization, and the World Bank. But the assumption that these agencies can bring minimal economic justice to the Third World in the next fifteen years is seriously contestable.

2. The statistics on global hunger continue to be appalling. Up to 800 million persons (one–eighth of humanity) are chronically malnourished. And the tragedy of famine playing out in Africa is not a one-time phenomenon due to a drought but a long-term reality attributable to the widespread erosion of fertile topsoil and an explosion of population all across Africa never before seen on any continent at any time in history. Children are the victims in special and tragic ways of man-

kind's failure to make decency available to every human being. UNI-
CEF regularly reminds us that 20,000 children die every day and that
10,000 of these youngsters could be saved if simple techniques for re-
hydration were available. Some church groups in the United States
identified with the pro-life or antiabortion positions regularly declaim
against the tragic 1.5 million abortions that occur annually in the
United States. But their support does not appear to be visible for the
very modest appropriations that according to James Grant, the head of
UNICEF, would result in the saving of the lives of 3,650,000 children
each year. Nor is there much concern among American churches for
the millions of children who will lead lives stunted by physical or men-
tal disabilities because adequate nutrition was not available in their
formative years. The churches of America, furthermore, have not ral-
lied to support the recommendations of the WHO, which has stated
that a one-time appropriation of less than $500 million would eradicate
the plague of malaria forever.

3. There are 350 million children of school age in the Third World
who have no school to go to. Illiteracy is not decreasing in the poorest
nations; it may be increasing somewhat.

All of these dreary statistics become even more heart-wrenching
when one contemplates the fact that the United States ranks only
fifteenth out of the seventeen nations that give financial aid to the Third
World. Church people who know of this embarrassing failure of the
United States may lament it, but there is no organized drive by the
churches of America to restore the United States to a top-rank position
among donors to the world's poor nations. The non-Christians in these
nations can hardly be expected to be impressed by the quality of Christian love in the rich nations.

The Third World looks at America, a nation that likes to describe
itself as an adherent of the Judeo-Christian tradition, and beholds an
annual budget for war approaching $300 billion and a budget for the
poor at home and abroad that is sharply in decline. The underdeveloped nations see 2.1 million persons in America in the armed forces—
the largest standing army in United States history. They have to conclude that either the churches approve of this massive threat of violence
or they are unable or unwilling to change it. The dozens of underdeveloped nations similarly saw the world's expenditures on the military soar to $660 billion in 1984—almost $2 billion per day—and again
wondered what the 130 million persons formally affiliated with Chris-

tian churches in America thought about this extraordinary phenomenon. It is elementary that this stupendous expense on weapons further impoverishes the poor. The arms race is, as the Holy See put it in 1976, "a crime against the poor."

There is active and deep concern for all of these issues within the churches of America. But no major group of believers is conspicuously identified as a religious organization that makes the alleviation of hunger and homelessness in the Third World its prime concern. The nearest approach to such identification came in the Catholic bishops' statement, "The Challenge of Peace," overwhelmingly ratified by the Catholic hierarchy in 1983. The forthcoming pastoral of the Catholic bishops on economics will also to some extent identify the bishops with the agony of the Third World.

But the fact is that the churches in America have silently acquiesced in the feeling pervasive in the United States that the prime duty of the government is to enhance the living standards of Americans and protect them against every conceivable threat from abroad. It is elementary that such a narrow view of the role of the American government is not compatible with Christianity or even with America's traditional view of its mission and mandate among the nations of the earth. But the churches, beset by their own problems of declining memberships and inhibited by the surrounding indifference or hostility to religion as a molder of public morality, have tended to deemphasize their mission as a global force and settle for a role that is more privatized than they desire or can justify.

Curiously, it was the fundamentalist churches and the religious right that broke out of that role in 1980. But their agenda concentrates on their own grievances about abortion, prayer in public schools, tuition tax credits for evangelical schools, and the new tolerance toward homosexuality. The mainline Protestant churches, challenged to justify some of their long-held positions, tended to put even further into the background whatever concerns they had for hunger in the Third World and related issues.

Will some religious groups in the next fifteen years recognize it as their right and duty to seek to direct the resources and energies of America to bringing elementary economic decency to the Third World? The answer to that question is not certain. But what is certain is that any interpretation of the Bible makes the present position of American Christians and the American government morally and scripturally intolerable. Now and in the year 2000, America will have only 5 percent of the total population of the world. It is presently consuming up to 40 percent of the world's resources. Even a modest cutback in the affluence of the United States would bring about a dramatic decline in the early deaths of children in the Third World. Even more startling is the fact that minor modifications of United States law and practice with respect to international trade could, without any loss of income to the United States, bring substantial improvements in the way millions of people live in Asia, Africa, and Latin America.

Even the most politically sophisticated religious groups in America have not developed their ideas very much on what they can do to alter the patterns of economic repression that are omnipresent in the Third World. Church groups have been articulate and aggressive on issues related to South Africa, human rights, and refugees, but the larger and admittedly more complex problems of America's overall policies with respect to the Third World have not attracted the attention of most church bodies. It is becoming clear, however, that America's relation to the Third World is the paramount and primordial moral issue involving government and religion in America today. It is infinitely more important than most if not all of the issues involved in the church-state cases before the Supreme Court. It is more important than, although to some extent inseparable from, the morality of the possession and use of nuclear weapons. It is, in short, the number one problem facing the world community, and hence the number one problem for the United States, the most powerful and the most affluent nation in the history of the world.

Theologians in the Third World are trying to teach Christians who live in conditions of economic repression how to be better Christians. One version of their teaching is called liberation theology. This is a doctrine designed to arouse within the souls of victims of economic injustice a sense of their own bruised dignity and a determination to organize, pray, and struggle to bring about their emancipation. The Holy See has stated that liberation theology is an authentic way of preaching the Gospel but has insisted that it must not be interwoven in any inappropriate way with Marxist analysis. The nature of that controversy has not emerged as yet, but the theologians and the people from Peru to the Philippines are trying to find a way by which millions of people can extricate themselves from institutionalized poverty and injustices.

The churches in America cannot be indifferent to this struggle. It is the struggle of fellow Christians whose lives and destinies can and will be profoundly influenced by policies chosen or rejected by the United States government. Consequently, religious organizations in America must be deeply involved in educating the American people as to their multiple responsibilities to the poorer nations. Religious groups must also be involved in helping the Congress and the White House adopt policies that will bring about liberation from those oppressive conditions that so afflict the people of the Third World.

Some may feel that this role goes beyond any traditional mission assumed or fulfilled by the churches in America. But such a negative approach fails to comprehend or reflect the prophetic role that the churches have always assumed in American life. The churches have spoken to and for the country with respect to dozens of moral problems. The churches have felt themselves to be the guardians and protectors of American morality. The churches have been America's moral architects and its conscience. They have tried to keep out of politics, but they have never said that they will not participate in the formation of the nation's moral policies.

It is agreed that sometimes the churches have gone too far; one example may be the enactment of the Volstead Act, the Eighteenth Amendment, an ill-conceived measure doomed to failure. But by and large America welcomes the initiative of the churches and other public interest groups in the formulation of laws and policies. No one wants the government in America to be inventing our moral standards. The government enforces the legal standards that have been passed by the legislatures. But it is the role of the churches and the people to decide on which moral ideals will become the law of the land.

In this traditional framework, therefore, it is not only the right but the duty of the churches to give guidance to the government as to the ways by which the power and might of the United States can be utilized to bring economic justice to the downtrodden and hungry in the underdeveloped nations. In view of the urgency of the problems, this role of the churches should have the highest priority. It is therefore depressing to see the disagreements among religious groups in the United States as to their role in offering guidance to the government concerning the Third World. Some churches have implicitly accepted the privatization enforced on them and do not want to be outspoken. Others have their own private agenda such as the restoration of prayers in school. Still others regularly speak out on social issues but seldom raise their minds or their concern beyond those issues that already have the attention of political liberals in the country.

The overwhelming problems that cannot be avoided by the Third World in the next fifteen years and the acute and appalling suffering now going on in those parts of the world make it clear that the Christians of America cannot do business as usual. The churches in America in the past have too often been silent. Examples of their silence are well known. They did little to prevent the sweatshops in thousands of mill towns in the nineteenth century. The churches did not stop the building of 30,000 nuclear weapons now possessed by the United States. Nor did the churches deter the growth of a Jim Crow society in the South or the development of all-black churches.

If the churches of America become involved in making recommendations about Third World economics, they will almost inevitably make mistakes. But at least they will be giving witness to the proposition that the Christians of America feel that they are their brothers' keeper because they are their brothers' brother. It is very difficult to say whether the churches of America could form a new alliance so that their considerable moral and political influence could be employed to help that part of humanity whose daily companion is hunger. But is it fanciful to think that the issue of the alleviation of economic justice and hunger—so elemental to every form of Christianity—might unite the Christians of America, even though they have differences on abortion, homosexuality, pornography, and tax support for church-related schools?

There is every indication that turbulence and political unrest will continue in the Third World before and after the year 2000. Millions of refugees may be moving across national borders looking for food. Political uprisings may be numerous, and wars like the conflict between Iraq and Iran and the chaos in Cambodia may multiply. The role of the United States in the next fifteen years and beyond will continue to be critical. Its foreign policy and its trade practices will determine in countless ways the quality of life for millions of people. The mistakes of commission and omission that have bedeviled American foreign policy in the past will continue. Clearly, a monitoring agency to guide the policies of the United States would be very useful. Is it unrealistic to think that such an agency could be organized or helped by the churches? It would not seem that there would be an objection on the ground that the religious bodies were interfering in the work of the state.

In the year 2000 and beyond, what will the world think of the role the churches in America played regarding the policies that the United States pursued in the last years of the twentieth century? Will the world look at history and conclude that the churches were silent in the face of global anguish? Or will history conclude that the churches were so involved in domestic church-state squabbles that they made little effort to use their collective influence to make America's foreign policy more moral and more generous? Or could it be that historians will look back and record that the churches of America came together in the last part of the twentieth century and, by persistent and united education and action, helped to bring about a foreign policy in the United States that so alleviated hunger and illiteracy in the Third World that those nations were well on their way to being just and compassionate societies?

Is that a dream that is too far-fetched? Not really. The moral and intellectual promise and potential of the religious bodies in the United States is enormous. Religious bodies have seldom if ever been united over a single issue, but the religious community in America possesses remarkable actual and political strengths. Traditional religious groups of every kind in America are a part of and are devoted to the uniquely religious character of the American government. Religion was a significant factor in the coming to the United States of some 50 million persons. The desire and determination to fight against political and economic tyranny have always been deep in the hearts of a people born from a revolution against a nation perceived to be a tyrant. The policy of containing Communism, adopted years ago as one of the main objectives of American foreign policy, derived in part from the hatred of tyranny. Now new forms of economic tyranny constitute an undeniable challenge to the United States. Unlike many forms of political oppression, economic injustice can be corrected and uprooted. It is a part of the American tradition—a tradition grounded in Christian teaching—that the United States will be a good Samaritan.

History may record that the churches in America have had more influence on public morality than in most modern pluralistic nations. The most visible triumphs for the churches are the abolition of slavery in 1865 and the enactment of the Civil Rights Act in 1964 and the Voting Rights Act in 1965. But there are many more triumphs, many unheralded or even unknown. The history of America has been filled with examples of the closest collaboration between government and religion. The ideals of the churches have become, to a remarkable degree, the morality of the government. That relationship is not about to disappear. Indeed, the religious right wants to take advantage of that relationship to have the government enact some measures it thinks are desirable as public policy.

Can the churches and the government bring about a collaboration from which there will emerge policies that will bring economic justice to the Third World? The churches have a great deal going for them because of the long-held aspiration of the American people to help other nations throw off tyranny and economic injustice. Archibald MacLeish put it well in these words: "There are those who will say that the liberation of humanity, the freedom of man and mind are nothing but a dream. They are right. It is a dream. It is the American dream."

Note

1. *Washington Post*, March 16, 1985.

Church Activism in the 1980s:
Politics in the Guise of Religion?

ERNEST L. FORTIN

By virtually all accounts, the most striking feature of present-day Christianity is the massive involvement of its leadership in the great social and political debates of our time. Three simple examples, chosen at random from three different continents, will illustrate the point. A few years ago, a French clergyman with whom I chanced to be living mentioned in the course of a heated discussion that, in his view, "the bourgeoisie have only one thing left to do: disappear!" The statement needed no further proof. It was self-evident. One had only to read the Gospel in order to be convinced of its truth. No decent person was at liberty to disagree with it. More recently, Denis Hurley, the Catholic archbishop of Durban, South Africa, who was indicted for his allegedly slanderous denunciations of police brutality, was cheered in his cathedral when, the day before the trial was scheduled to begin, he declared, "The Gospel is political!" Lastly, on the occasion of John Paul II's first visit to South America, a missionary stationed in Peru was quoted as saying that his experience in that country had finally taught him what Christianity was all about: to defend the weak and the poor, abolish misery, and wage war on injustice. Strange as it might have sounded at other moments in history, the reforming zeal to which these assertions bear witness is shared in varying degrees by a growing number of Christians who have come to view their faith as an enterprise dedicated to eradication of the evils that plague human existence by transforming society along more or less leftist lines.

There is reason to suspect that what my European friend, the South African archbishop, and the Peruvian missionary took to be the timeless (if only newly discovered) wisdom of the Gospel is little more than the distilled "wisdom" of the sages in whom, to speak like Goethe, "the mirrored age reveals itself." It is unlikely that such ideas would ever have become as popular as they are had they not been borne on the wings of powerful intellectual currents that have shaped the thinking of the modern church; and it is even less likely that theologians and religious activists of various stripes would have succumbed to them so readily had they not themselves been psychologically prepared for them by a long line of secular thinkers who, knowing that they could not do away with Christianity altogether, sought to achieve their goal by redefining it in political terms or reducing it to a political phenomenon. Liberation theology, which has been making the headlines of late, is only one manifestation of the new syndrome, and perhaps not the most important one at that, for it too is but a bastardized product of the less visible ideological forces that have been at work in our society for quite some time.

Rome's obvious uneasiness, not to say displeasure, with this type of theology and John Paul II's repeated warnings against the danger of mixing religion and politics suffice to remind us that not everybody in the church is happy with the direction in which some of its lesser representatives have been moving. Yet the Pope's own stance and posture in regard to these matters often comes across as ambiguous. His public speeches in different parts of the globe are meant to have an impact on the lives of the nations at which they are aimed, and much of what he has said over the years in defense of social justice, world and local poverty, the role of labor, free trade unions, and the sharing of wealth has very definite political overtones. Because of the liberal thrust of many of these statements, some widely read analysts have gone so far as to brand him a socialist. Others find him inconsistent insofar as he strenuously objects to any clerical meddling in politics while he himself never passes up an opportunity to lecture party chiefs and ruling juntas about violations of human rights, religious freedom, and human dignity. Still others have pointed to what they call his "geopolitical ambivalence," accusing him of using one set of standards when speaking to his fellow Poles and a different set when addressing, say, Latin American audiences.

Much the same could be said of the American bishops, who have been outspoken in their criticism of the regime but refuse to admit that their pronouncements have anything specifically political about them. Many of them in fact were astonished and not a little dismayed when, a few years ago, the *New York Times Magazine* ran a feature article boldly entitled "America's Activist Bishops: Examining Capitalism."[1] To make matters worse, the front cover showed a group of three purple-clad bishops huddled in a private conference on which, judging from the grim look on their faces, the fate of the world seemed to hinge.

Are the ecclesiastical authorities confusing religion and politics when, in their official capacity, they lobby for or against defense systems, economic programs, and a host of domestic or foreign policies over which the country is divided at the present moment, or is there some higher ground on which their intervention in temporal affairs conceivably could be justified? What finally distinguishes the political from the nonpolitical, and where does one draw the line between them? This question, which is the one I would like to address, has yet to receive a clear answer. My tentative suggestion is that the church's present stand on this matter makes complete sense only within the context of our typically modern understanding of society and the peculiar brand of apolitical politics that goes hand in hand with it. I shall begin with a brief account of what I take to be the fundamentally nonpolitical orientation of the New Testament, turn from there to a discussion of the manner in which its teaching was reinterpreted in the modern period, and finally take up the larger issue of the relationship between church and state as it presents itself in the light of recent developments.

The New Testament and the Political Life

Anyone who reads the New Testament from the perspective of an outsider, without any previous knowledge of the centuries-old tradition that came out of it, is bound to be struck by its blatant disregard for the realities of the political life. The Gospel all but opens and closes with a denial of the temporal or political nature of Jesus's messiahship. The temptation scene in the desert, which constitutes the immediate preparation for everything that follows in the text, shows Jesus refusing to change stones into bread and rejecting Satan's offer to place him at the head of all the kingdoms of the world if he would but worship him (Matt. 4:1–11). And when, toward the very end, Jesus is summoned by Pilate to respond to the charge that he had tried to make himself king, his answer takes the form of an emphatic proclamation to the effect that his kingship is not of this world (John 18:36).

Much of what transpires between these two scenes is a concerted effort to show that Jesus had come not to restore the old kingdom of Israel but to establish a new kind of kingdom, one that was spiritual in nature and totally divorced from the political concerns that animated his disciples. By way of example it might help to take a quick look at Mark's account of the Transfiguration on Mount Tabor, where for the only time in the Gospel Jesus reveals himself in all of the radiant splendor that belongs to him as the son of the Father (Mark 9:2–10). Characteristically, the event is set within the context of the celebration of the Feast of Tents, which lasted six days and during which, in accordance with Jewish custom, the Messiah to come was symbolically enthroned. Next to him appear Moses and Elijah, who represent the law and the prophets respectively, and thus sum up the entire pre-Christian dispensation. Contrary to all expectations, however, Moses follows Elijah and takes second place to him. It is not Moses, the founder of the nation and the mediator of its covenant, than whom none was thought to be greater (Deut. 34:10; cf. Num. 12:1–8), but the persecuted and suffering prophet who prefigures most directly the mission of the new Messiah.

This was a radical novelty, and that is why explaining it to the disciples proved to be such an arduous task. There is no evidence that any among them understood it during Christ's lifetime, and even when he appears to them after his resurrection, we still find them asking, "Lord, is it now that you are going to restore the kingdom to Israel?" (Acts 1:6). Unlike the Judaism in which it finds its preparation, Christianity is in essence not a political religion but an altogether different type of religion—one in which the individual's relationship to the transcendent deity is mediated not by a divine law or one's participation in a covenant that binds a group of people together as members of an earthly community but by faith in the person of the living Christ. Nobody to my knowledge has stated the crucial difference between the two religions more succinctly and more perspicaciously than Gershom Scholem:

> Judaism, in all its forms and manifestations, has always maintained a concept of redemption as an event which takes place publicly, on the stage of history and within the community. It is an occurrence which takes place

in the visible world and which cannot be conceived apart from such visible appearance. In contrast, Christianity conceives of redemption as an event in the spiritual and unseen realm, an event which is reflected in the soul, in the private world of each individual, and which effects an inner transformation which need not correspond to anything outside. Even the *civitas dei* of Augustine, which within the confines of Christian dogmatics and in the interest of the Church has made the most far-reaching attempt both to retain and to reinterpret the Jewish categories of redemption, is a community of the mysteriously redeemed within an unredeemed world. What for the one stood unconditionally at the end of history as its most distant aim was for the other the true center of the historical process, even if that process was henceforth decked out as *Heilsgeschichte*. The Church was convinced that by perceiving redemption in this way it had overcome an external conception that was bound to the material world, and it had counterpoised a new conception that possessed higher dignity. But it was just this conviction that always seemed to Judaism to be anything but progress. The reinterpretation of the prophetic promises of the Bible to refer to a realm of inwardness, which seemed as remote as possible from any contents of these prophecies, always seemed to the religious thinkers of Judaism to be an illegitimate anticipation of something which could at best be seen as the interior side of an event basically taking place in the external world but could never be cut off from the event itself. What appeared to the Christians as a deeper apprehension of the external realm appeared to the Jews as its liquidation and as a flight which sought to escape verification of the Messianic claim within its most empirical categories by means of a non-existent pure inwardness.[2]

Despite its apolitical nature, the New Testament presupposes the existence of civil society and recognizes its necessity. Since Christians were not to form a nation of their own and were not given a law by which such a nation might be governed, it was assumed that they would continue to live under the laws of the particular societies to which they happened to belong and in accordance with them. In this sense, the New Testament view is perhaps best described as transpolitical rather than apolitical. Christians were not asked to turn their backs on their fellow human beings and could not reasonably be accused, as they often were by their pagan critics, of misanthropy or hatred of the world. On the contrary, it was their God-given duty to dedicate themselves to the welfare of others, with whom they were expected to share a common life even though they themselves were called to a loftier personal ideal. The knowledge acquired through revelation was inseparable from the love of neighbor. Therein lay the problem, for it was inevitable that at some point or other the demands made on them by their faith would come into conflict with those of a civil society that is always less than perfect and whose laws are never completely just.

On that score, the New Testament has no firm or fully developed teaching. In some instances, it takes a positive view of civil society, enjoining Christians to obey their rulers, "honor the emperor," pay taxes, be "subject for the Lord's sake to every human institution," and "maintain good conduct among the Gentiles." Since temporal rulers have been divinely ordained for the punishment of wrongdoers, to resist them was to resist the will of God himself, at the risk of incurring his wrath (Rom. 13:1–7; cf. 1 Pet. 2:11–17). Other texts strike a different, more negative note. They remind these same Christians that they are not to be "conformed to this world" (Rom. 12:2) and that they have to "obey God rather than men" (Acts 5:29). Some of them even take an extremely dim view of the Roman Empire, identifying it with the harlot "seated upon the seven hills" and "drunk with the blood of the saints and the martyrs of Jesus" (Rev. 17:9 and 18:24).

How these conflicting strains could be harmonized is a question that the New Testament never expressly deals with and that does not appear to have been a major concern of the sacred writers, partly, one surmises, because all or most of them were convinced that the end-time was near. If the world as we know it was about to pass away, and if Christians had to "deal with it as though they had no dealings with it" (1 Cor. 7:31), there was no need to be preoccupied with one's ambiguous relationship to political institutions, however good or bad they may have been.

This explains why it has always been so difficult to derive a coherent plan of action from the pages of the New Testament alone. The pagan Celsus, the first great philosophic critic of the new faith, concluded that, if Christians were consistent, they would go into the wilderness and die without having had any children,[3] which is exactly what Antony, the father of Christian monasticism, did after walking into a church one day and hearing the words: "Go, sell what you possess and give to the poor, and you will have treasure in heaven; and come, follow me" (Matt. 19:21). Others, like the Spaniards of the Golden Age, chose instead to conquer the world, making "disciples of all nations [and] baptizing them in the name of the Father and of the Son and of the Holy Spirit" (Matt. 28:19), whether they liked it or not.

The one text that seems to offer at least the beginnings of a solution to the problem at hand is the famous maxim "Render to Caesar what is Caesar's and to God what is God's" (Matt. 22:21; Mark 12:17; Luke 20:25), which became a *locus classicus* of sorts in the political literature of the Middle Ages, but its scope is limited by the narrow context in which it occurs. Christ obviously had no intention of enunciating a general principle that could be applied to a variety of similar situations. His sole purpose was to elude the trap laid for him by his enemies, in this instance the Pharisees and the Herodians, who, although bitter rivals, had found an opportunity to make common cause against him. Their specific question was whether Jews ought to pay the tribute demanded by the emperor. If Christ answered yes, he was a collaborationist and hence a traitor to the Jewish nation; if no, he was a zealot who deserved to be punished for his refusal to comply with Roman law. The rejoinder was a clever one. It reminded the Pharisees that by using imperial currency they were availing themselves of the benefits of Roman rule and were thus bound to give the emperor his due; and it reminded the Herodians that their collusion with the Romans did not dispense them from the service owed to God. From an argument such as this one, few general conclusions can be drawn. Far from resolving the issue of church-state relations, it brings it into sharper focus by highlighting the inevitable tension between divine and political authority. Oscar Cullmann's observation that Christ was merely telling the state that it should not be "more than the state"[4] misses the point altogether, since the state was conceived as a unitary whole commanding the undivided allegiance of its citizens. To say that one should render to Caesar what was Caesar's meant nothing to someone who was convinced that everything was Caesar's. Such a claim may not have been fully enforceable, for history knows of no higher regime that has ever realized its ambition of becoming a total way of life; but it was a claim that the Roman rulers were not ready to give up.

For all its far-reaching political implications, the New Testament has no genuine political teaching of its own and, while it is not unaware of the harsh necessities of the social life, it evinces hardly any interest at all in them. As Thomas Aquinas would later say, the justice of which it speaks is not the justice of this world, sufficiently known through the first principles of natural reason, but the "justice of the faith," *iustitia fidei*,[5] which has been given to us not to solve the problems of civil society but to lead us to the blessedness of eternal life.

It is therefore no mere accident that the internal history of Christianity, in contrast to that of Judaism or Islam, traditionally has been dominated by doctrinal rather than legal or juridical preoccupations. Justification was achieved not through the performance of such righteous deeds as might be prescribed by the law but through faith. In the absence of a divinely mandated social organization, Christian unity was secured by a commonality of belief. Orthodoxy was thought to be more important than orthopraxy, and what one held as a believer took precedence over one's actual way of life, which could vary greatly from one place to another. Accordingly, theology and not jurisprudence became the highest science within the community and the locus of its liveliest debates, all of which tended to focus on points of doctrine rather than on points of law. As has rightly been observed, no other religious group has placed a greater premium on the purity of doctrine or has been so much on its guard against heresy. For this reason, the Church's authority was always understood to be first and foremost a spiritual authority. Nowhere in the Christian tradition does one encounter the kind of concern for the perfect law or the perfect social order that is so prominently displayed in both Judaism and Islam.

The Politicization of Christianity

In light of everything that has been said thus far, it comes as something of a surprise that the leaders of the Christian churches suddenly should be so eager to invade the political domain not simply to demand the freedom required for the exercise of their proper functions, which they have always enjoyed in this country, but to influence public legislation and governmental policy on the premise that work for social justice is a "constitutive dimension" of their ministry, on a par with the preaching of the word of God and the celebration of the sacraments. And it comes as an even greater surprise that they should insist on grounding their own proposals in the New Testament, which is mostly silent about such matters. A good case in point is the Catholic bishops' much-publicized 1983 pastoral letter on war and peace and their more recent (1986) letter on the American economy.[6] I leave it to others to take issue with the specific positions taken in these two documents, as well they might, and concentrate only on the dangers in the attempt to develop from the sacred text a doctrine that has no solid basis in it.

The simple fact of the matter is that the New Testament has no clear or consistent teaching on war, makes no effort to deal with any of the complex moral issues that it raises, and does not even show any distinct awareness of the existence of these issues. It is tempting, of course, to argue that war is ruled out by the commandment to love, but that inference is not necessarily warranted and is never drawn by the sacred writers themselves. Indeed, from the same commandment one could just as easily come to the opposite conclusion; it is surely not a sign of love to allow unjust aggressors to oppress or tyrannize one's friends, fellow countrymen, and others for whose safety one is responsible. Moreover, there appears to be at least an implicit recognition of the legitimacy of war under certain circumstances in the Letter to the Romans, which makes it plain that rulers have been ordained by God for the express purpose of inflicting his wrath on evildoers (Rom. 13:4), something they could hardly do without resorting to force and, if need be, military force.

As for the few New Testament texts that could be invoked in support of nonviolence, they are either beside the point or subject to interpretation in the light of other texts that run counter to them. Christ, who occasionally speaks with soldiers, does not rebuke them for their profession or urge them to lay down their arms but actually commends them for their righteousness. Nor is it true to say that the commandment "Thou shalt not kill" contains an implicit condemnation of war, for that commandment is really a modified version of the more precise "Thou shalt not murder" and blurs the distinction between killing and murder, which the original text is careful to maintain. The soldier, unlike the murderer, is not someone who takes the law into his own hands. He does not exercise the right of private judgment or try to determine for himself who ought or ought not to be allowed to live. There is a difference. Christ does say that "he who lives by the sword will die by the sword" (Matt. 26:52); yet, since he himself died a violent death without ever having held a sword, the maxim appears to be somewhat less than universal in scope. To be sure, Christians are urged to "turn the other cheek" (Matt. 5:39) and to requite evil with good (cf. Rom. 12:17–21), which is not necessarily a bad idea; but these principles, too, take on a different meaning when viewed within the context of one's relations with all of one's fellow human beings. A slap on the cheek with the back of one's hand was a common insult that ordinarily invited some form of retaliation. In such instances, the offended person might well choose to forgive rather than stand on his honor, especially

if he has only himself to think about; but it is easy to imagine other
instances in which the same forbearance would do more harm than
good. Significantly, the situations envisaged in the New Testament are
one-on-one situations rather than situations in which the welfare of
third parties, to say nothing of entire communities, is at stake. They
have nothing to do with the mode of behavior that is in order when
conflicts of a general nature threaten to erupt. It is surely a sign of the
fundamental ambiguity of the New Testament concerning these matters
that, with seemingly equal right, radicals at both ends of the political
spectrum have been able to appeal to it to defend pacifism or to justify
their involvement in revolutionary activities.

Similar remarks could be made about the New Testament attitude
toward wealth and poverty. It would be strange, to say the least, if
Christ, who had no money of his own and who seems to have depended
so much on the hospitality of his rich friends, had been opposed to
riches as such. The Gospel frequently alludes to the poor, but its overwhelming emphasis is on spiritual rather than material poverty, in
keeping with a tendency that was already present in the Old Testament
and that stretches back to at least the seventh century B.C. The key text
on this subject is Zephaniah 3:12, where, perhaps for the first time, the
word *poor*, which originally designated a social class, is invested with a
religious and ethical meaning. The poor in this new sense are the pious
and humble people who place their trust in God rather than in political
schemes or worldly goods. Neither in this tradition nor in the New
Testament tradition that grows out of it is there any suggestion that
economic poverty could be abolished or that the lower classes ought to
be elevated at the expense of the wealthier ones. If the poor are really
closer to God, I suppose one should think twice before robbing them
of their poverty. In any event, most of the New Testament passages
relating to poverty, the Canticle of Mary among them (Luke 1:46–55),
are barely more than paraphrases of Old Testament texts whose meaning has been further spiritualized. The parable of Lazarus and the Rich
Man (Luke 16:19–31) is just another example of the same mentality. If
the Gospel writer had been intent on condemning wealth, he could
hardly have missed this unique occasion to do so. Yet one looks in vain
for any such condemnation in the text, which instead leaves us with the
impression that there is a good and a bad use of wealth, just as there is
a good and a bad use of poverty. The poor person who lives in envy of
his rich neighbor does not thereby prove his moral superiority to him.

Besides, if wealth itself were the issue, one would have a hard time explaining why, after his death, Lazarus was rewarded by being placed in the bosom of Abraham, who is said to have been "very rich in cattle, in silver, and in gold" (Gen. 13:2).

Finally, even when the New Testament does speak about the economically poor, it is less from their point of view than from the point of view of those who are called upon to help them. The New Testament, it seems, is more interested in the internal dispositions of the doer (or nondoer) of the just or merciful deed than in the social condition of its recipient. The Good Samaritan is the one who is indebted to the man who had fallen among thieves for the privilege of serving him, and not vice versa. In the words of an ancient Christian writer, who was merely echoing what others before him had said, "What kind of people are we if, having received everything from God, we refuse to give anything to others?"[7] Succinctly stated, one does not bear witness to the truth of the Gospel and the love of God by closing one's heart to the victims of misfortune or the plight of the needy.

Precisely because the New Testament has no political agenda of its own, Christian theologians concluded long ago that the knowledge required to deal with such problems would have to come from other sources, and that is why they turned to political philosophy. Decisions of a political nature became matters of prudential judgment, duly informed by general principles of justice and a proper regard for the demands of the common good. Few if any absolutes could be invoked to resolve the complex problems political leaders are likely to confront. In each instance, one had to look for the solution that was most conducive to the general welfare. The assumption was that what was best in itself was not necessarily best at this or that particular moment, or for this or that particular group, and hence no single solution or plan of action would ever accommodate all of the unforeseen and unforeseeable circumstances in the midst of which decisions affecting the life of a nation have to be taken. The highest court of appeal was the natural law, which gained new prominence in the twelfth century, once the task of sorting out ecclesiastical laws from civil laws had been accomplished. As originally conceived, however, the natural law was a subtle instrument, to be used in a manner that took into account the high degree of contingency that surrounds human actions. The inflexibility associated with natural law in the minds of our contemporaries is a more recent phenomenon, traceable to the changes it underwent in the sixteenth and

seventeenth centuries under the impact of the new philosophic and
scientific theories of that period. To appreciate the distance that separates its earlier exponents from the later ones, one has only to observe
that, by the time we reach Grotius, the four short articles that Thomas
Aquinas devotes to the problem of war in the *Summa Theologiae* had
expanded into a mammoth 800-page quarto.

If, then, the New Testament contains so few political imperatives, so
little that bears any direct relationship to the political life, what impels
so many church leaders to look to it for practical guidance in these
matters? What accounts for the sudden surge of interest on their part
in such mundane matters as military strategy, government planning,
economic rights, and the like, often at the expense of other topics that
were formerly considered more worthy of their attention and more appropriate to their calling? As I have already intimated, part of the answer may be found in a series of earlier developments, whose full
impact has only recently been felt within the churches. Two authors in
particular deserve to be singled out as having had a determining influence in this respect. One is Spinoza, who denied that there was any
theoretical teaching whatsoever to be extracted from the Bible and reduced the whole of its content to a moral teaching. That moral teaching
is summed up in two words: justice and charity. Charity itself is taken
only in its crudest and most superficial sense as that virtue by which
one is inclined to help the needy. It is not intrinsically linked to those
moral virtues that perfect individuals in themselves and concerns only
their relations with others. The argument was all the more clever as it
served a twofold purpose: once accepted, it could help put an end to
religious persecution, which Spinoza attributed to the traditional Christian emphasis on doctrine as distinguished from morality; and, more
importantly in Spinoza's view, it could be used to reclaim for philosophy the independence it had lost as a consequence of its subordination
to theology.

The second great fountainhead of our currently most fashionable
ideas is Rousseau, the author most responsible for setting modernity
on the course it was to follow with all kinds of detours down to our
time. Only two related facets of Rousseau's thought need to be retained
for present purposes: his reinstatement of religion as the true bond of
society and the source of its vitality and his so-called politics of compassion, both of which are of a piece with his radical egalitarianism. As

we know from the *Profession of Faith of the Savoyard Vicar* and other texts, the religion in question is a religion without dogmas, or with only the simplest of dogmas. It is essentially a civil religion, but one that differs from the civil theology about which the authors of antiquity had spoken in that it is meant to close off any access to a higher or nonpolitical realm. The politics of compassion serves the same goal by calling for a greater equalization of social conditions through a restructuring of the entire political order. People were no longer to be rewarded on the sole basis of what they contributed to society; their poverty was a sufficient title to whatever benefits they could expect to receive from it. The neediest elements of society were the ones most deserving of its attention, and every disadvantaged citizen had an immediate claim on the compassion and benevolence of his fellow citizens. In the name of egalitarian democracy, the poor had become, to use a more recent expression, the object of a "preferential option."[8]

The dramatic impact of Rousseau's views is observable throughout the vast literary, sociological, and philosophic production of the nineteenth century. In Saint-Simon, the founder of French socialism, the interest in the poor had grown to the point of excluding virtually every other concern. Taking his cue from Rousseau, Saint-Simon started from the belief in God but cleared theology of all dogma. His famous essay *The New Christianity* is predicated on the principle that "the whole of society ought to strive toward the amelioration of the moral and physical welfare of the poorest class" and that it should "organize itself in the way best adapted to the attainment of this end."[9] A similar note is struck in Victor Hugo's poetic masterpiece, *The Legend of the Centuries,* whose sketch of the progress of the human conscience from its biblical origins onward climaxes in the glorification of a family of lowly fishermen, "The Poor People," in mid-nineteenth-century Brittany.[10]

The rise of Neo-Thomism as the dominant force in Roman Catholic theology did much to stem the tide of modernity within the church and gave a more conservative tone to the bulk of its theological speculation. However, in its initial stages the return to Thomas Aquinas was motivated primarily by practical rather than theoretical reasons. What rendered the Thomistic position attractive to Christians who were struggling to adjust to the conditions of postrevolutionary European society is that it recognized the naturalness of the political order and was thus able to supply the philosophical premises by which the church could relate to it. From the use of Thomas Aquinas by nineteenth-century theologians came what is now referred to as the "social teachings" of the Catholic church. Yet there is ample evidence to show that the solution these theologians finally came up with was more a compromise with modern thought than a genuine reappropriation of the principles that had governed premodern Christian thought.

Be that as it may, the collapse of Neo-Thomism in the wake of Vatican II paved the way for the emergence of a variety of more recent schools, Christian Marxism and liberation theology among them, in which the characteristic nineteenth-century amalgamation of religious and social concerns attains its most acute form. Both of these movements share with earlier Christian thought the view that the Gospel alone is incapable of furnishing the guidance needed for the successful management of political affairs. The difference is that the new theology looks to Marx rather than to classical philosophy for that guidance. This is certainly true of Christian Marxism, but it is equally true of liberation theology, however eager it may be to reject abstruse philosophical speculations associated with European thought and to pass itself off as a native Latin American product. As the late Gaston Fessard has so well shown, there is a straight line that goes from the works of the defrocked Italian priest Giulio Girardi to those of Gustavo Gutierrez, the presumed originator of liberation theology and still its most respected spokesman.[11] Granted, Girardi is cited only twice in Gutierrez's *A Theology of Liberation,* but a careful scrutiny of this work, such as Fessard's, reveals a much closer connection between the two authors than Gutierrez himself has thus far been willing to acknowledge.[12] The point at issue is not whether the liberationists are right or wrong in criticizing the abuses of governmental power or the exploitation of the masses by powerful and selfish elites, but whether the systematic use of Marxist categories to diagnose the evils of contemporary society does not implicitly commit the user not only to the narrow conception of justice embodied in these categories but to the philosophical materialism from which they appear to be inseparable. This, I take it, is the ground of the reservations expressed, for example, in Cardinal Josef Ratzinger's *Instruction on Certain Aspects of the Theology of Liberation.*[13] Baptizing Plato and Aristotle, which is what the Church Fathers and their medieval disciples attempted to do, not without some difficulty, is one thing; baptizing Marx may turn out to be quite another.

The Church and Social Justice

This still leaves us without an answer to the more general question: How can the church censure these and similar movements as misguided attempts to politicize Christianity even as it continues to issue statements that are fraught with unmistakable and sometimes momentous political implications? Is the church contradicting itself, or do its leaders really believe that their own incursions into this troubled area are situated on a plane that transcends that of politics?

One convenient way to approach the problem is through the notion of social justice, which in the last fifty years or so has become a standard feature of official church documents as well as of much of the theological literature of our time. Unfortunately, the history of that novel expression has yet to be written, and its meaning remains vague. Taparelli d'Azeglio, the Roman Catholic theologian who is credited with having coined it, is anything but explicit in his discussion of it in his *Saggio teoretico di diritto naturale appoggiato sul fatto (Theoretical Essay on Natural Right)*, an immensely popular nineteenth-century work that first appeared in 1840 and was subsequently translated into most of the major European languages.[14] Even a cursory glance at the book reveals that its author was more learned than profound, more eclectic than consistent, and more muddled than clearsighted. In fairness, one has to admit that he inherited an unenviable situation when, at the age of fifty and without any previous experience, he was appointed to a chair of moral theology in Sicily. Seminary life had been severely disrupted by the French Revolution, scholasticism had ceased to be a living tradition, and the only manual at his disposal was that of the Swiss jurist Burlamaqui, of Rousseauean fame, which was ill suited to his purpose. The only alternative was to write his own manual, which turned out to be a blend of Thomistic, Lockean, and traditionalist ideas in the midst of which there appears, seemingly out of nowhere, something labeled "social justice."

Taparelli's nineteenth-century followers, who by then had acquired a better knowledge of the premodern tradition, were understandably bewildered. To which, if any, of the three hitherto known forms of justice—legal, distributive, and commutative—was social justice related? The shrewdest among them leaned toward the first, but with some reluctance since the resonances did not appear to be the same. Besides, to call justice "social" seemed redundant, inasmuch as justice had always been regarded as the social virtue par excellence—unless, as proved to be the case, it could be shown to designate a reality that is not covered by any of the older views of justice. Still, it is doubtful whether the notion would have stuck had it not fallen on soil that was already well prepared to receive it.

Justice in this new sense, one is tempted to say, is not a virtue at all, in that it has more to do with social structures than with the internal dispositions of the moral agent. Its proper object is not the right order of the soul but the right order of society as a whole. It shares with early modern liberalism the view that society exists for the protection of certain basic and prepolitical rights, and it radicalizes that view by combining it with an emphasis, stemming ultimately from Rousseau, on the need for a greater equalization of social conditions as a means of guaranteeing the exercise of those rights. It thus takes for granted that social reform is at least as important as personal reform and that the just social order depends as much on institutions as on moral character. It keeps the Lockean notion of labor as the origin of property but looks upon the accumulation of wealth as a form of exploitation of the poor by the rich few and, hence, as the root cause of the inequities that pervade modern western society. Accordingly, it calls for either a radical redistribution of material resources or, short of that, the establishment of a system that reduces as much as possible the distance separating the social classes. Its immediate goal, in short, is to produce happy rather than good human beings. Taparelli himself, who in this instance at least is fairly consistent, went so far as to claim that all human beings had a right to happiness and not just to the pursuit of virtue. In the final analysis, there is one and only one just social order, whose broad outlines are prescribed in advance and therefore are not a proper object of deliberation on the part of wise and prudent legislators.

Are the churches or their representatives engaging in politics in the guise of religion when, in the name of Gospel, they call for the eradication of the systemic injustices of society through the reform and, if need be, the overthrow of the structures in which these evils are supposedly embedded? For better or for worse, this is what some theologians who would reduce the Christian faith to a program of political and social liberation are in fact doing. Whether it is also what the Pope and the bishops are up to is doubtful. Yet they too, it seems, have unwittingly or uncritically acquiesced in the new trend and think they can exclude from the realm of politics proper certain decisions that were once regarded as preeminently political. It used to be that there were two noble alternatives to the political life: revealed religion and philosophy. We are now given to understand that there is a third, specifically moral and thisworldly in character and all the more attractive because it addresses itself to all decent human beings, whether or not they are religiously inclined.

At the risk of ending with what may appear to be a hopelessly vague generalization, I would simply ask whether the modern rights theory that lies at the root of so much of what our church leaders have been saying lately is compatible with the stress on duties or virtue that is typical of the older approach to these matters. The controversies over this question in recent years suggest that the answer to it is not clear, or that there is a certain lack of clarity in the minds of those who have been trying to answer it. There is nevertheless some comfort to be taken in the thought that in all but the rarest of instances, clarity about theoretical issues has never been the hallmark of our political and religious leaders.

Notes

1. Eugene Kennedy, "America's Activist Bishops: Examining Capitalism," *The New York Times Magazine*, August 12, 1984.

2. Gershom Scholem, *The Messianic Idea in Judaism* (New York: Schocken Books, 1971), pp. 1–2.

3. Origen, *Contra Celsum*, translated with an introduction and notes by Henry Chadwick (Cambridge: Cambridge University Press, 1953), 8.55, p. 493.

4. Oscar Cullman, *The State in the New Testament* (New York: Scribner's, 1956), p. 90.

5. Thomas Aquinas, *De Veritate*, qu. 12, a. 3, ad 11.

6. National Conference of Catholic Bishops, "The Challenge of Peace: God's Promise and Our Response," *Origins* 13, no. 1 (May 19, 1983): 1–32; "Economic Justice for All: Catholic Social Teaching and the U.S. Economy," *Origins* 16, no. 24 (Nov. 27, 1986): 409–55.

7. Caesarius of Arles, *Sermons* (New York: Fathers of the Church, Inc., 1956), 25.1, pp. 127–28.

8. See, for example, the Catholic bishops pastoral on the U.S. economy, notes 16, 52, and 85–91, pp. 411, 418, and 421–22.

9. Claude-Henri de Saint-Simon, *Le nouveau christianisme, Oeuvres complètes*, vol. 3 (Geneva: Slatkine Reprints, 1977), pp. 117, 177.

10. Victor Hugo, *La légende des siècles*, LII: "Les pauvvres gens" (Paris: Garnier, 1964), pp. 700–7.

11. Gaston Fessard, *Chrétiens marxistes et théologie de la libération* (Paris: Lethielleux, 1978), esp. pp. 413–21.

12. Gustavo Gutierrez, *A Theology of Liberation* (Maryknoll, N.Y.: Orbis Books, 1973), pp. 271, 275.

13. The text of the *Instruction*, issued by the Congregation for the Doctrine of the Faith, may be found in *Origins* 14, no. 13 (Sept. 13, 1984): 193–204.

14. Luigi Taparelli d'Azeglio, *Saggio teoretico di diritto naturale appoggiato sul fatto* (Palermo, 1840, and Rome, 1855), vol. I, bk. ii, ch. 3: "Nozioni del diritto e della giustizia sociale," Rome edition, pp. 220–32.

Some Thoughts on
Conservatism and Religion

WERNER J. DANNHAUSER

The distinction between conservatives and liberals, between right and
left, remains significant. Many political theorists and most political
practitioners decry the need for labels, but the labels themselves remain
useful, helping us to describe reality. It may well be the case that in
today's United States most citizens think of themselves as being in the
middle. But if we understand the center geometrically, as a point without dimensions, we must once more differentiate between left centrists
and right centrists, between liberals and conservatives. The differences
between them can be fuzzy, but they are nevertheless real, and the two
groups certainly have a history, possibly even a nature. As to history,
the distinction between the left and the right appeared as part of the
French Revolution, and even today conservatives continue to harbor
doubts about that revolution while liberals continue to view it with
nostalgic enthusiasm. Thus, too, conservatives excel in seeing the dangers of Communism but may be slow to understand fascism; liberals
understand the evils of fascism but can be soft on Communism.

The most marked difference between liberals and conservatives concerns religion. Conservatives tend to believe, liberals to doubt. Atheism
may be almost coeval with human thought. After all, there must have
been fools almost as soon as there were human beings, and the Bible
tells us, "The fool hath said in his heart: 'There is no God.' "[1] One does
well, however, to distinguish between atheism as a permanent possibility for individuals and atheism as a political force, even as Edmund

Burke did: "Boldness formerly was not the character of Atheists as such. They were even of a character nearly the reverse; they were formerly like the old Epicureans, rather an enterprising race. But of late they are grown active, designing, turbulent and seditious."[2] Burke wrote those words in 1791. He held the French Revolution responsible for unleashing atheism, making it fashionable, moving it from the privacy of philosophical speculation into the arena of public life. This linking of atheism with the left is by no means confined to enemies of the revolution like Burke. It is echoed by most of its friends, like Marx.

Burke's perspicacious remarks point to the fact that different stances toward religion on the part of leftists and rightists can be observed on the level of practice as well as on the level of theory. Theory influences practice; different theories lead to different practices. To speak of atheism's becoming fashionable is to speak of political movements espousing it, and those political movements originally belonged to the left exclusively. In the nineteenth century, liberals and radicals came to view religion simply as superstition and to opt publicly for mankind's emancipation from it. They equated religion with fear and began to think of freedom from fear as a basic freedom. When Hobbes wrote of "the Kingdom of Darknesse"[3] he was referring, overtly at least, primarily to the Catholic church, but that phrase soon came to signify the whole realm of religion. The left, marching under the banner with the magic word *Enlightenment* written on it, promised to bring relief from that darkness. Radicals and liberals can be said to have forced the right into a defensive posture. The word on the right's banner became *Tradition,* and therewith began some difficulties in the relationship between conservatives and religion, difficulties this chapter attempts to articulate.

As conservatives, lovers of tradition, we praise the old, what is hallowed by time and usage; our mockers have a good point when they define a conservative as one who is against anything being done the first time. We identify the old with the good. Much can be said for that procedure, especially that it is much easier to tell what is old than what is good. Moreover, as believers, we have faith in the God of Creation whose eternal being precedes our puny existence. As the primal source of goodness, our God must be revered as being simultaneously the oldest and the best.

At this point, our confusions and difficulties begin. Either out of ignorance or because of darker promptings, we continually mistake what is merely old for what deserves reverence as the oldest. Let a habit or an institution grow ancient, and we conservatives may well succumb to the temptation of going beyond respecting it toward sanctifying it. I will cite an example from the religious tradition with which I am most familiar, Judaism. I grew up to think of Judaism and monogamy as inextricably linked. To be more specific, I "knew" monogamy to be one of the laws to be found in our Book of Laws, the Bible. I had, of course, read about Abraham's having Hagar as a concubine and Jacob's marriage to both Leah and Rachel, but for some reason that made no impression on me. As do many conservatives, I read the Bible selectively. It was enough for me to "know" that the Bible said "Therefore shall a man leave his father and his mother, and shall cleave unto his wife, and they shall be one flesh."[4] Only much, much later did I learn that monogamy did not unequivocally become Jewish law until the twelfth or thirteenth century.[5]

Let us then concede that we conservatives frequently think of certain practices as having been in place "from time immemorial" when they are only somewhat dated. Our traditionalism does not always serve us well. Again and again, we are embarrassed by the fact that tradition seems to preserve rather promiscuously or incoherently. It has carried down to us ridiculous superstitions as well as lofty songs. Transmitting so much, it also transmits much that is contradictory, and we often are unable to decide between rival traditions without leaving the plane of the traditional.[6]

Nor do our troubles end there. Conservatives soon discover they are not the only ones who seek to justify themselves by appealing to the old. Thus the partisans of the French Revolution, later to become known as the left, judged and condemned the ancien régime in taking their bearings by something more ancient: They appealed to nature. Using nature as standard, they understood it as prior to human artifacts. The state of nature precedes the state of civil society just as natural rights precede civil rights. Moreover, nature is usually seen as the uncreated creative force, but what then differentiates nature from God?

Conservatives have not exceled in answering this question or even in dealing with the dilemmas it poses. Instead they have resorted to various more or less unsatisfactory strategies. For example, they have tried to distinguish between left-wing worshippers of nature and right-wing worshippers of God. Such a distinction may once have generated insight, but as time passed it began to distort reality rather than to chart it. The left abandoned nature as a standard in favor of history, and one could find about as many nature-oriented conservatives as God-oriented conservatives. Even when it pointed to real divisions in the real world, the distinction proved unfortunate. After all, it strikes common sense as ludicrous to try to comprehend nature as a left-wing phenomenon, even as it seems stupid as well as blasphemous to consider God as a right-wing phenomenon. We ought to take our bearings not only by what is left and right but by what is above.[7] Where, then, does that leave conservatives?

Sometimes we argue for a synthesis of that part of our heritage stemming from Jerusalem—God—and that part of our heritage stemming from Athens—nature. However, on close inspection, most syntheses turn out to be imperfect, with a clearly dominant principle, or volatile, or both, and the synthesis between Jerusalem and Athens proves no exception. That is why so many great thinkers of the past have been able to use Jerusalem as a stick with which to beat Athens or Athens as a stick with which to beat Jerusalem.

Sometimes we argue that the differences between Athens and Jerusalem may be real but that they do not matter all that much for all practical purposes. Yet it would be easy to show that it can matter on a daily basis whether we take our bearings by a rational nature rather than a holy God. Moreover, it will not do to pretend that no difference exists between nature's God and God's nature. Jerusalem and Athens share an idea of transcendence, and what they have in common goes a long way, but it does not go all the way. Moreover, where one finds a salutary agreement, one also notes the absence of anything to provide conservatives with a firm and unique basis for their heritage. In the United States both liberals and conservatives admire the Declaration of Independence as being good and as being their own. It is not altogether obvious that conservatives have a better claim in this respect than liberals.

In their general contests with liberals, conservatives do not always fare as well as they might. On the level of political practice one must remember that the label affixed to them by John Stuart Mill caught on and still haunts conservatives today: They became known as the stupid party. On the level of political theory one must ponder the fact that in the last analysis Edmund Burke, the patron saint of conservatives, strikes one as less profound, less philosophical, than his adversary

Jean-Jacques Rousseau, the patron saint of the left. In our time thoughtful conservatives have conceded as much.[8]

One suspects that conservatives could improve their reputation as well as their perceptions by rethinking some of their views on religion. Such rethinking might begin with an appreciation of the inevitable tensions between religion and politics. When the Sea of Faith recedes, we may have to face nihilism, but it does not follow from this that harmony accompanies the Sea of Faith at high tide. Our dreams of a harmonious past do violence to the past, encourage a general sappiness of the mind, and detract from our ability to deal with the present and the future. Probity and prudence both dictate that as nearly as possible we remember history as it really was. We must then think of crusades, inquisitions, the struggles of Popes against kings, religious wars. We must heed Machiavelli's implicit linking of piety with pious cruelty.[9] We must remember that believers believe in a Fatherland above all fatherlands and that the city of man can never equal the city of God.

Some who do heed the historical record argue that the tension exists not between politics and religion generally but between politics and Christianity in particular. Sometimes they dream wistfully of a civil religion that might replace Christian universalism. Frequently, they have in mind the ancient *polis* in which the gods who were worshipped were the gods of the city. However, the most authoritative work on the "religion, laws and institution" of the ancient city does not altogether support these dreams of harmony. Fustel de Coulanges understands religion as "the constituent principle of the ancient family,"[10] and the interests of the family need not coincide with the interests of the *polis*. Dissension unto death can be present even when the family in question is the royal family. The quarrel between Antigone and Creon serves as the most enduring example of this truism.[11]

It may nevertheless be true that Christianity exacerbates the conflict between religion and politics. Gibbon argued that it destroyed "the greatness of Rome," leading to its decline and fall. Discussing the religious scene before the advent of Christianity, Gibbon wrote, somewhat wistfully, "The various modes of worship, which prevailed in the Roman world, were all considered by the people, as equally true; by the philosophers, as equally false; and by the magistrate, as equally useful. And thus toleration produced not only mutual indulgence, but even religious concord."[12] It will be noted that in this passage of surpassing eloquence, Gibbon distinguishes between the truth and the utility of religion. We conservatives owe it to ourselves, and not only ourselves, to meditate on the complexities attending this distinction. Is religion true because it is useful? Is religion useful because it is true? Might religion be both false and useful?

Confronting these and kindred questions, we chance upon another area of inquiry we conservatives have not exceled in investigating. Sometimes instinctual conservatism too blithely asserts religion's usefulness on the ground that it, and only it, makes people good. That assertion should crumble in the presence of the first decent atheist in our midst, and many of us know many decent atheists (as well as indecent believers), but it has managed to survive all empirical evidence. A common stratagem consists of denying not the decency of the atheist but the atheism. One contends that the decent may well be believers without knowing they believe, the proof of their belief being their decency. It scarcely needs saying that such reasoning (if one can call it that) does not honor conservatives and that it never attempts to understand atheists as they understand themselves.

A more estimable line of argument maintains that religion is useful not because it makes human beings good but because it makes them happy. This contention, too, entails difficulties. One would first have to deal with those who contend that the relief from religion is tantamount to a relief from unhappiness because it takes away the fears of human beings. Moreover, conservatives must be careful in pursuing this train of thought that they do not uncover an altogether problematic—at least for them—distinction between being happy and being good.

Conservatives have a better case when we consider social and political life as a whole. One need not deny the existence of nonbelievers who are virtuous or those who attain serenity without belief in God. We now have enough historical experience with secularism to declare that the waning power of religion in modernity has not made people either happier or better, let alone happy and good.

Those who continue to decry the monstrous deeds committed in the name of the Christian God must come to terms with the crimes committed by the godless in one century. The pious cruelty of the past has yielded to the impious cruelty of our time, and in this respect at least we moderns have outdone the ancients. No inquisitor and no crusader can match the crimes perpetrated by Hitler and Stalin within the living memory of many of us.

It may be objected that in the United States we need not beat our breasts about the crimes of Stalin and Hitler. After all, we did our share to defeat Nazi Germany and to contain the Soviet Union. What is more, if a decency index could be constructed, we would not have to fear comparison with any Age of Faith. That argument has something to be said for it—and against it. It fails to gauge the continuing role of religion in our lives, and it fails to admit that we are neither happy nor good in today's United States.

In political life, the immediate and middle-range problems always take priority. We simply cannot afford the luxury of fretting about our mortal or immortal souls when we must cope with deficits at home and the Soviet Union abroad. Now let us for a moment conceive of what is well-nigh inconceivable: The Soviet Union transforms itself into a more benign regime that no longer threatens us, and we perfect our economic system so that it deals flawlessly with poverty, business cycles, and the budget. In that happy event, would we be or even become happy or good? We would not. President Carter was almost certainly right when he diagnosed us as suffering from a national malaise.[13] Our souls are sick.

In the last analysis, then, the argument for the utility of religion proves powerful. Our virtues surely need various kinds of buttressing and may even need cosmic support. It remains as true as it ever was that man does not live by bread alone. Mankind needs spiritual sustenance. We need things above us we can adore, that to which we can bow down in good grace. Religion is useful because it fills human needs that nothing else has proved able to fill. Experiments in secular living have proved unsuccessful. The separation of church and state in the United States has caused problems; besides, it does not abolish religion. To repeat: The case for the utility of religion proves powerful.

Once we agree as to religion's utility, however, we must still face the disquieting possibility that religion might be useful even though it is false—and the much more disquieting possibility that it is useful *because* it is false. We dimly refer to such possibilities whenever we speak of salutary or nurturing myths. Plato's Socrates calls them noble lies; Nietzsche calls them holy lies.[14]

Conservatives have no great trouble admitting that false religions may lead to true morality. It is not particularly disturbing to think of, say, a tribe whose god of the wind teaches gratitude. The trouble comes when conservatives are asked to question the truth of their own (good) religion. In attempting to defend the truth of the true faith, they rely too often and too much on tradition, and they are forced to fudge the difference between the part of the tradition stemming from Jerusalem and the part stemming from elsewhere.

The saints in the tradition sustaining us agree that the truth was revealed at Mount Sinai, some maintaining that it was elaborated—perhaps transcended—on the Cross. But the philosophers in the tradition sustaining us lead toward skepticism. Thus a reading of the *Euthyphro* leads to the impression that piety is a substitute virtue. One might even suspect that the gods exist only for those who are not intelligent enough to think in terms of the ideas.

The gods, to be sure, are not God, so one can try to understand classical philosophy as the highest and best thought of which human beings are capable without the benefits of the revealed truth stemming from Sinai and Jerusalem. Plato and Aristotle thus are understood as the precursors of the Judeo-Christian tradition, which supersedes their thought in decisive respects. Such an argument may or may not carry conviction in regard to Greek philosophy, but it surely does nothing to explain the lack of belief of those who had the opportunity to deal with the Bible.

It can be said with a good deal of plausibility, though with a great deal of exaggeration, that the whole tradition of philosophy is strong in praising the utility of religion and weak in claiming truth for it. One thinks of Averroes, and Avicenna, of Machiavelli's treatment of Moses,[15] of Hobbes, Locke, and their successors. They praise the usefulness of religion, but their tributes to its veracity are likely to remind one of the presence of censorship and the absence of deep conviction.

Even when philosophers think of God with all due seriousness, it is likely to be more in terms of a cosmic force or a prime mover than the biblical God. How does one adore a God who resembles, say, electricity more than the source of all mercy and justice? How does one pray? Considerations of this sort led Blaise Pascal, after his mystical experience of 1654, to the determination to devote his life to the "God of Abraham, God of Isaac, God of Jacob, not of philosophers and scholars."[16]

Pascal's testimony ought to be invaluable to us. We may suspect nonbelievers of vested interests when they claim the whole philosophical tradition as their own, but Pascal impresses us with the profundity of his faith. Moreover, his credentials include an indisputable mastery of mathematics and science as well as indubitable insights into the thought of the ancients. We therefore owe him our attentiveness when he dismisses all of philosophy as a diversion from the good life and when he troubles us by characterizing as atheists so many great thinkers whom we do not, at first sight, consider as such.[17] In this respect, we ought also to study Martin Luther's argument with Erasmus.[18] Pascal and Luther together offer powerful testimony to the effect that philosophy tends toward nonbelief. Moreover, they take to task a number of thinkers who cannot be excused on the ground that they had no opportunity to hear the good news from Jerusalem.

As citizens of the United States, we should pay special heed when men the stature of Luther and Pascal bring the whole tradition of philosophy under the suspicion of atheism. Time has cast no veil over the origins of our country, which were decisively influenced by the teachings of that tradition. Recalling Locke's influence on Jefferson and the number of times the authors of the *Federalist Papers* cite Montesquieu, we do no injustice to the founders when we think of them as part of the Enlightenment. Their pronouncements on religion strike us as more prudential than enthusiastic. Thus George Washington said in his Farewell Address:

> Of all the dispositions and habits, which lead to political prosperity, religion and morality are indispensable supports. In vain would that man claim the tribute of Patriotism, who should labor to subvert those great pillars of human happiness, these firmest props of the duties of Men and Citizens. . . . A volume could not trace all their connexions with private and public felicity. Let it simply be asked where is the security for property, for reputation, for life, if the sense of religious obligation *desert* the oaths, which are the instruments of investigation in Courts of Justice? And let us with caution indulge the supposition, that morality can be maintained without religion. Whatever may be conceded to the influence of refined education on minds of peculiar structure—reason and experience both forbid us to expect, that national morality can prevail in exclusion of religious principle.[19]

Washington here—and elsewhere—says much more about the utility of religion than about its truth. Most of the other leaders of our revolution echo him in this respect. In private they may well have speculated more boldly than in public about the possibility of a self-subsistent morality, but they appreciated the role of religion in producing civility. They surely opposed a frontal assault on the fund of faith bequeathed to them by Puritanism, though our hindsight makes us wonder whether they were concerned enough about its depletion.

Writing in the middle decades of the nineteenth century, Tocqueville found America's fund of faith to be in sound condition. Among us conservatives his testimony counts for a great deal. Liberals, too, claim him, and *Democracy in America* contains enough insights to go around, but we conservatives have good reason for thinking him one of our own. He reassures us by writing of affinities between religion and democracy, by demonstrating the role religion plays in shoring up our two great principles of liberty and equality, and above all by showing that the separation of church and state can be beneficial to state and church. Yet he too causes us to wonder about the strength of his religious belief. We do not quite know what he means by Providence, for example, and we cannot help but notice that in crucial passages he too emphasizes not the truth of religion but its usefulness.[20]

The nineteenth century's most portentous statement about religion comes from Tocqueville's younger contemporary, Nietzsche, who announced to the world that "God is dead."[21] The primary meaning of his statement is that religion has lost its power over human life, its social force. Thus a proof of God's existence would not refute Nietzsche, and a proof of God's nonexistence would not corroborate him. Nietzsche meant to teach us that the utility of religion was at an end because the belief in its truth was at an end.[22]

A variety of forces had conspired to produce a decisive turning point in human affairs, according to Nietzsche. The higher criticism of Spinoza had made the acceptance of revelation immeasurably more difficult. Christianity had developed a conscience so strict and tender that it turned on Christianity itself. Modern science had painted a persuasive picture of a chaotic universe. Not only God is dead; all gods are dead, all transcendent truths and standards.

One does not refute Nietzsche's pronouncement by pointing to the persistence of belief; Nietzsche never doubted that. Nor is one done with him when one can show that belief is not only widespread but pervasive. In Gallup polls, well over 90 percent of all Americans may profess to believe in God, but those results say nothing as to the depth of the belief that Americans profess.

In our century many a celebration of religious revival has turned out to be premature, as the revival in question has turned out to be quite shallow. In today's America we are more likely to be surprised by a prominent man's religious fervor than by his atheism. And the believers are more likely than before to keep their belief compartmentalized, so as to assure us that for the most part they are just like everybody else. In other words, unbelief sets the tone for belief.

Too many conservatives have failed to come to terms with Nietzsche's thought, dismissing it as an embarrassing attempt to outflank them on the right. But the challenge he represents will not go away. Nietzsche went far beyond Burke, who held out for the hope for a time when atheism might cease to be fashionable. Nietzsche postulated an irreversible loss of naïveté in western civilization. To put the matter crudely, he argued that the cat of atheism was out of the bag. The meanest capacities could now learn that religion was a myth; and when a myth is exposed as a mere myth, it can no longer provide a unifying horizon.

Too many conservatives whose own belief is weak or nonexistent, who will admit privately that religion is "for the troops," continue to try to teach the catechism to those troops, forgetting that the latter by now have been thoroughly exposed to the Enlightenment and its lessons. They probably overestimate the credulity of the many, just as they probably underestimate the snobbishness of the few.

On a deeper level, one can say that too many conservatives betray their own superficiality when they pretend that the truth of religion does not matter much because man is simply a religious animal with religious needs. If God is dead, or if He never existed, and man is nevertheless a religious animal, we must face the abysmal truth that man is so structured that reality can offer no fulfillment to his highest hopes or deepest yearnings. Man is the animal that must hallucinate to be happy. But at this point conservatism ends and nihilism begins. If man is the hallucinating animal, the world is a chaos. But conservatism's fundamental assertion has always been that human order is part of a cosmic order.

Psychologists of the phenomenological or existentialist persuasion might accuse conservatives of practicing denial when it comes to Nietzsche's thought, and they would have a point. It probably would be simpler to say that conservatives think of religion as their own and thus recoil from any perceived threat to it. They may not appreciate Nietzsche properly, but they understand correctly his call for a candid atheism. Nietzsche asks them to surrender something near and dear to them, so they turn away.

The same proprietary interest in religion makes them too reluctant to admit that today religion is very often on the other side. It will not do to characterize the Ayatollah Khoumeini and his followers as a right-wing phenomenon (that may be just as well). In England, the Church of England is in many respects to the left of the conservatives. In South America, liberation theology comes on as strong and resilient. And in the United States religious enthusiasm fuels not only the Moral Majority but the efforts of Jesse Jackson. Instead of thinking in terms of left and right when it comes to religion, one can try to distinguish between orthodoxy and gnosticism, as does Irving Kristol,[23] but then one must wonder whether conservatism has not failed to assess gnosticism correctly.

The above criticisms of conservatives frequently have assumed an accusing tone, so it is proper to mention that they apply above all to myself, a conservative. Since breast-beating possesses limited utility— and limited truth—let me hasten to add that a chapter dealing with liberals and religion would have to contain more criticism, more strictures, than this one.

When all is said and done, conservatives today, it seems to me, have closer ties to religion than do liberals. The latter are too closely linked to materialism, humanism, and scientism to have an elective affinity to religion. We conservatives do have just that, which is why we must become more adept in its defense.

What can we do? We must eschew the tendency to pay mere lip service to religion; we must stop being pious about piety. Today those who seek to enhance the utility of religion must grapple with its truth. That is easier said than done. Fortunately, it is also beyond the scope of this chapter. Two reflections must suffice. First, today it seems clear that defenders of the truth of religion had better not dwell on the proofs of the existence of God. Those proofs do little to convince. A ceaseless encounter with the Bible offers, in all probability, a more fruitful road. Second, we will not necessarily be judged by our failure to succeed in the work cut out for us, but we will surely be held responsible by our failure to accept the task. We learn from the tradition we seek to buttress: "It is not thy duty to finish the work, but thou are not at liberty to neglect it."[24]

Notes

1. Psalm 14:1.

2. Edmund Burke, "Thoughts on French Affairs," in *Reflections on the French Revolution* (New York: E. P. Dutton & Co., 1951), p. 314.

3. Part 4 of *Leviathan* is entitled "Of the Kingdom of Darknesse," and its first chapter (44) defines the meaning of the phrase.

4. Gen. 2:24.

5. See "Monogamy," *Encyclopedia Judaica*, s.v.

6. See Leo Strauss, *Natural Right and History* (Chicago: University of Chicago Press, 1953), pp. 81–120. My general debt to the thought of Leo Strauss is beyond specific acknowledgment.

7. This formulation appears in a different concept in Joseph Cropsey, *Polity and Economy: An Interpretation of the Principles of Adam Smith* (The Hague: Martinus Nijhoff, 1957), p. x.

8. The works of Allan Bloom and his students, Marc Plattner and Joel Schwartz, should be consulted. For an evaluation of conservative elements in Rousseau's own thought, see Arthur Melzer, "Rousseau's Mission and the Intention of His Writings," *American Journal of Political Science* 27 (May 1983): 294–320.

9. Niccolas Machiavelli, *The Prince*, chaps. 17, 18.

10. Fustel de Coulanges, *The Ancient City* (Garden City, N.Y.: Doubleday Anchor Books, n.d.), pp. 40–42.

11. In *Antigone*, compare Creon's case for obedience to the polis (11.162–210) with Antigone's case for obedience to higher laws (11.450–70).

12. Edward Gibbon, *The Decline and Fall of the Roman Empire* (New York: Modern Library, n.d.), pp. 25–26.

13. See *New York Times*, July 23, 1985, p. 1.

14. Plato, *Republic*, 4141–415e; Nietzsche, *Antichrist*, sect. 56.

15. See *The Prince*, chaps. 6, 26.

16. Blaise Pascal, *Pensees*, trans. A. J. Krailsheimer (Baltimore: Penguin Books, 1968), p. 309.

17. Ibid., pp. 72–74, 243. Pascal's scattered but intriguing comments on Montaigne and Descartes merit special attention.

18. See Martin Luther, "The Bondage of the Will," in *Martin Luther: Selections from His Writings*, ed. John Dillenberger (Garden City, N.Y.: 1961), pp. 166–203, esp. pp. 318–19.

19. *The Washington Papers*, ed. Saul K. Padover (New York: Universal Library, 1955), pp. 318–19.

20. Alexis de Tocqueville, *Democracy in America*, trans. George Lawrence (Garden City, N.Y.: Anchor Books, 1969), p. 444: see also Marvin Zetterbaum, *Tocqueville and the Problem of Democracy* (Stanford, Calif.: Stanford University Press, 1967), chap. 1.

21. Nietzsche, *Thus Spoke Zarathustra*, Prologue, sect. 2.

22. Can God be born again? Nietzsche does think in these terms, and one can even speculate that he envisions such a rebirth. That need not concern us here, for the new God would not be biblical, nor would the world in which belief in Him might be useful remotely resemble our own.

23. See Irving Kristol, "The Spiritual Roots of Capitalism and Socialism," in *Capitalism and Socialism: A Theological Inquiry*, ed. Michael Novak (Washington, D.C.: American Enterprise Institute for Public Policy Research, 1978), pp. 2–6.

24. *The Living Talmud: The Wisdom of the Fathers*, trans. Judah Goldin (New York: Heritage Press, 1957), p. 58.

Religious Roots of the Rights of Man in America

JERRY H. COMBEE

The form of Religion . . . decides that of the State and its Constitution.
—Hegel

I

Leo Strauss introduced his 1949 lectures, which became *Natural Right and History*, by reciting from the Declaration of Independence a passage

frequently . . . quoted, but, by its weight and its elevation . . . made immune to the degrading effects of the excessive familiarity which breeds contempt and of misuse which breeds disgust. "We hold these truths to be self-evident, that all men are created equal, that they are endowed by their creator with certain unalienable Rights, that among these are Life, Liberty, and the pursuit of Happiness." The nation dedicated to this proposition has now become, no doubt partly as a consequence of this dedication, the most powerful and prosperous of the nations of the earth. Does this nation in its maturity still hold these "truths to be self-evident"? About a generation ago an American diplomat could still say that "the natural and divine foundation of the rights of man . . . is self-evident to all Americans." At about the same time a German scholar could still describe the difference between German thought and that of western Europe and the United States by saying that the West still attached decisive importance to natural right, while in Germany the very terms "natural right" and "humanity" have now become almost incomprehensible . . . and have

lost altogether their original life and color." . . . What was a tolerably
accurate description of German thought . . . [earlier] would now appear
to be true of Western thought in general. It would not be the first time
that a nation, defeated on the battlefield and, as it were, annihilated as a
political being, has deprived its conquerors of the most sublime fruit of
victory by imposing on them the yoke of its own thought.[1]

The Nazis lost the battle of bullets, but they won the war of ideas.
The same relativism, existentialism, and historicism that supported
fascist ideology has become the new rationale, or perhaps we should
say rationalization, for democracy. At the time of the founding, government by consent rested upon the belief in absolute moral and meta-
physical truths with quite specific theological content; and until quite
recently, the conviction that every person is the direct creation of God,
with equality, freedom, and rights, constituted the very foundation of
American civilization. Today democracy is defended as the only system
compatible with the truth that there is no truth and with every individual's infinite right of free choice. One contemporary theorist has expressed the new logic of democracy in typical fashion: "If . . . decisions
on public policy always involve matters of preference, the ultimate
'rightness' of which cannot be demonstrated, then what rational justification can there be for including as a matter of principle the preferences of some citizens while excluding the preferences of others?"[2] The
new religious right and the Moral Majority have stirred a storm of controversy because they are unwilling to play democracy by the new rules
of the game. How well these forces understand the old logic of democracy may be debated, but clearly the Jerry Falwells harken to an earlier
day when absolutist claims constituted the case for democracy.

It has become fashionable to cite Calvin Coolidge for the cause of
supply-side economics.[3] Less well known is his surprisingly astute
understanding of the religious roots of American political principles.
President Coolidge believed that

in its main features the Declaration of Independence is a great spiritual
document. When we come to a contemplation of the immediate conception of the principles of human relationship that went into the Declaration
of Independence we are not required to extend our search beyond our
own shores. They are found in the texts, the sermons, and the writings of
the early colonial clergy who were earnestly undertaking to instruct their
congregations in the great mystery of how to live. They preached equality

because they believed in the fatherhood of God and the brotherhood of men. They justified freedom by the text that we are all created in the divine image, all partakers of the divine spirit.[4]

The original rationale for American democracy was essentially religious, not so much a theory as a theology, and though not the same as Christianity, certainly rooted in and related to it—a "civil religion," if you will, but not necessarily any less true for being civil and very close to what Rousseau, democracy's greatest theoretician, described in Book 4 of *The Social Contract*. Leo Strauss suggested that understanding anew the "problem of natural right," "a matter of recollection rather than of actual knowledge," requires that we "become students of what is called the 'history of ideas.'"[5] But we must study more than the history of ideas of philosophers. Perhaps it is "to Hobbes we must turn if we desire to understand the specific character of modern natural right,"[6] in particular influences upon later philosophers of natural right. But for the sources of the popular mind and the consensus of opinion expressed in the Declaration, we must also turn to more plebeian philosophers and to the English Protestant sects broadly known as Puritans. Facts not so long ago common knowledge to schoolchildren (and to readers of Tocqueville)—facts about the Pilgrims and the Massachusetts Bay Puritans, about such colonial American heroes as Thomas Hooker of Connecticut and Roger Williams of Rhode Island—suggest that rather than speculations of allegedly atheistic philosophers, what Coolidge called "the spiritual insight of the people"[7] produced the Declaration of Independence. The basic political ideas contained in that document, long before any philosophical attempt to articulate them, were proclaimed and practiced by the English Protestants who colonized North America in the 1620s and 1630s and understood these precepts as the logical implications of Christianity for civilization.

We can see Puritan/Protestant maxims at their purest in the applications made in colonial America, where, as far as the settlers were concerned, a "state of nature" existed. In England, where an existing order and tradition had to be confronted, either revolution or accommodation was necessary. In America, where circumstances permitted the founding of entirely new orders, the Puritans could write upon a blank slate.

America is a land of many foundings; each colonial beginning was a "founding." Understanding the meaning of 1776 requires more than reflection upon the thoughts of the founding fathers, or the views of reputedly irreligious philosophers who influenced them. Tocqueville, believing that even as "the entire man is, so to speak, to be seen in the cradle of the child," so "the growth of nations presents something analogous," held that "not an opinion, not a custom, not a law, . . . not an event" of America "is upon record which the origin of that people will not explain. . . . In the English colonies of the North, . . . main ideas that now constitute the social theory of the United States were first combined. The principles of New England spread. . . . The civilization of New England has been like a beacon lit upon a hill."[8]

The story begins in seventeenth-century England.

II

No work of art summed up the spirit of an age better than John Bunyan's *Pilgrim's Progress,* one of the most widely read English-language books of all time. What Homer was to the Greeks, Bunyan became to the English-speaking peoples through this theological odyssey of a man who dared to ask, "What shall I do?" Bunyan's poem was a perfect allegory for seventeenth-century England, a whole nation of "pilgrims" living out the individualistic logic of the Protestant Reformation.

By the end of the seventeenth century, this pilgrimage had taken England far down the road to religious and civil liberty. After the trials and tribulations of civil war and revolution, the principles of religious toleration (though still limited) and government by consent (still limited, too) were firmly established in the laws of the country. The time was ripe for philosophy: "As to the individual, everyone is the son of his own time, and therefore philosophy is its time comprehended in thought."[9] Just at that moment John Locke summed up what now seemed self-evident truths valid for all people in all times and places. His work, like Bunyan's, was nearly universally acclaimed; Locke expressed in incomparable fashion what thinkers already believed.

Earlier in the century, however, when the outcome of the struggle for freedom in England seemed much in doubt, some sought more promising conditions for freedom in the wilderness of America. One group of a hundred or so made their journey in 1620, and in history, poetry, oratory, sermon, and song have come to be known simply as the Pilgrims.

In the reign of Henry VII, the English Reformation began with the break from Rome, but that only made the king "the pope in his own dominions" and "the right of correcting errors of religious faith . . . a branch of the royal prerogative." England therefore stopped short of the Protestant principle of the priesthood of believers, according to which "Every man . . . [is] his own priest . . . directly in the hands of the Almighty, with no other mediator than the Eternal Wisdom, with no absolution from evil deeds but by repentance and a new life," with "the individual . . . under God alone . . . independent of pope, bishop, priest." As long as English monarchs claimed unlimited power and therefore control over religion, they would be at odds with the essential Reformation tenet of the priesthood of believers, the highest "expression of the liberty of the individual." "No bishop, no king," was how James I saw it, and English history proved him correct. "In an age when political questions were enounced in theological forms," astute princes desiring to sustain despotic power could not be expected to write the very "inscription on the gate through which the more advanced of the human race were to pass to freedom."[10] It was through that gate that the Pilgrims passed to freedom.

Whereas many Puritans preferred to stay in the Church of England, wanting only to purify it of resemblance to the Church of Rome, the Pilgrims were separatists who would have no part of the Anglican established church. Separatists believed that every church congregation should be separate and independent from every other church, from any and all denominational officials, and entirely self-governing. They considered each church a little democracy—one man, one vote—with all final decisions by majority vote of the congregation. The requirement of church separation, independence, and democracy they deduced from the priesthood of believers was to the separatists very much a cardinal doctrine. "Everyone is made a king, priest, and prophet, not only to himself but to every other, yea to the whole," is how separatist John Robinson, pastor to the Pilgrims and advocate of the power of the people in churches, put it.[11] The Pilgrims got their idea of political liberty and equality from their ideas of religious liberty and equality. What they preached and practiced in the church, they proclaimed and applied in the polity when Providence (or what some would call fortune) gave them the opportunity to found an entirely new political order.

A storm blew their *Mayflower* to the coast of Massachusetts, not Vir-

ginia, and hence outside the limits of their patent and beyond the jurisdiction of the London Company. They recognized the king's authority,
but neither he nor his agents were there. Being without effective civil
government, the Pilgrims were in what Locke more than sixty years
later, in the *Second Treatise of Civil Government,* would call the *state of
nature:* a "state of perfect freedom to order their actions and dispose of
their possessions and persons as they think fit, within the bounds
of the law of nature, without asking leave or depending upon the will
of any other man." They were "men living together according to reason, without a common superior on earth with authority to judge between them."[12]

In Locke's analysis, however, the state of nature tends to turn into a
"state of war" because of those whom he called the "quarrelsome and
contentious," who would rather steal and kill than work and produce.[13]
Aboard the *Mayflower,* the Pilgrims, almost as if they were playing out
Locke's script, heard certain "discontented and mutinous speeches that
some . . . amongst them had let fall . . . that when they came ashore
they would use their own liberty; for none had power to command
them, the patent they had being for Virginia, and not for New England,
which belonged to another government, with which the . . . [London]
Company had nothing to do."[14]

The Pilgrims had to find a way to establish an effective civil government, and they did so in perfect Lockean fashion: through consent.
Locke would write more than a half-century later that "men being . . .
all free, equal, and independent, no one can be . . . subjected to the
political power of another without his consent. The only way whereby
any one divests himself of his natural liberty and puts on the bonds of
civil society is by agreeing with other men to join and unite into a
community for their comfortable, safe, and peaceable living one
amongst another, in a secure enjoyment of their properties and a greater
security against any that are not of it."[15] Forty-one adult males went
into the cabin of the *Mayflower* and, as if they had the *Second Treatise*
open before them, so closely did their actions parallel Locke's principles, drew up and signed what Winston Churchill called "one of the
most remarkable documents in history, a spontaneous covenant for political organization"[16]—the Mayflower Compact: "We . . . covenant
and combine ourselves into a civil body politic, for our better ordering
and preservation . . . to enact, such just and equal laws, ordinances,
acts, constitutions, and offices . . . convenient for the general good . . .
unto which we promise all due submission and obedience."[17]

The Mayflower Compact, as President Coolidge observed, "proclaimed the principle of democracy."[18] It assumed that the people had to consent before a legitimate government could be set up with the right to be obeyed. Noticing the close congruence with social-contract theories of political legitimacy and obligation, John Quincy Adams considered the Mayflower Compact

> perhaps the only instance in human history of that positive, original social compact which speculative philosophers have imagined as the only legitimate source of government. Here was a unanimous and personal assent by all the individuals of the community to the association by which they became a nation. The settlers of all the former European colonies had contented themselves with the powers conferred upon them by their respective charters, without looking beyond the seal of the royal parchment for the measure of their duties. The founders of Plymouth had been impelled by the peculiarities of their situation with deeper and more comprehensive research.[19]

America's "national historian," George Bancroft, described the Mayflower Compact as "the birth of popular constitutional liberty": "The middle ages had been familiar with charters and constitutions; but they had been merely compacts for immunities, partial enfranchisements, patents of nobility, concessions of municipal privileges, or limitations of the sovereign power in favor of feudal institutions."[20]

The Pilgrims hit democratic milestone after milestone: (1) for a time they practiced direct democracy; (2) after they grew too large for direct democracy to be practical, they established functioning institutions of representative democracy; and (3) they adopted a body of laws called the "General Fundamentals" that were "in effect a constitution for the colony and even equivalent to a Bill of Rights . . . the first Bill of Rights in America."[21] "In the cabin of the 'Mayflower' humanity received its rights," wrote Bancroft.[22] And this prototypical liberal democracy was established in 1620, twelve years before the birth of Locke and twenty years before the publication of Hobbes's first political writing.

How could such a group, sprung from the mass of the common people, unmarked by any special attainments in education, with no philosophers among them, display political sagacity so advanced for the age? Historian John S. Barry wisely advises against flattering "our ancestors by ascribing to them motives different from those which they themselves professed" and reminds us that they were "endowed with no singular prophetic vision, and . . . [claimed] no preternatural political sagacity." He attributes the Pilgrims' political accomplishments to common sense: "they adopted that course which commended itself to their calm judgment as the simplest and best." He explains the fact that "their compact was democratic" with the suggestion that "self-government is naturally attractive to the mind" and "spontaneously resorted to in emergencies."[23] Nevertheless, we must still ask why, in the whole course of human history, is there practically no precedent for what the Pilgrims did? If it was all due to common sense, it was a sense not so common hitherto. Something must have caused the eyes of the Pilgrims to be open and receptive to such singular, simple propositions.

In trying to understand the Pilgrims, the most vital fact to remember is the supreme importance they attached to religious liberty. They considered the most important religious liberty of all to be what the born-again Christian experiences—what Christ meant when He declared, "if ye continue in my word, then ye are my disciples indeed; and ye shall know the truth, and the truth shall make you free" (John 8:31–32). The importance to Christians of inner freedom and the life beyond caused Rousseau to conclude that Christians therefore care nothing for their condition in this life: "Christianity preaches only servitude and dependence. Its spirit is over-favourable to tyranny, and the latter always draws its profit from that fact. True Christians are made to be slaves! They know it, and care little, for, in their eyes, this brief life counts for nothing."[24] What Rousseau and other political critics of Christianity have missed is that this "soul liberty," as it used to be called, makes a person want religious liberty on the outside, too—the exterior liberty to live and worship according to the dictates of his or her conscience. It was the longing of one man, Martin Luther, to have the free exercise of religion that started the Protestant Reformation. The same yearning drove the Pilgrims on from England, to Holland, to America.

The Pilgrims' desire for religious liberty put them at odds with the absolutist, divine-right English monarchy. A government that will admit no limit on its power necessarily will claim the right to infringe upon the free exercise of religion. Individuals seeking religious freedom, therefore, necessarily become proponents of limited government; they claim that the power of government is legitimately limited in the area of life most important to them, religion. The quest for religious liberty thus merges into a quest for political freedom. As President Coolidge observed:

The people who laid the foundation of our institutions had seen a great searching out of minds in the sixteenth century . . . [when] there had been put forth in matters of religion . . . the principle of private judgment. A remarkable body of men held to this theory with a tenacity which no persecution was able to shake. Along with it went the complementary doctrine of the direct contact of the individual with the Almighty . . . the standards of intellectual freedom and religious liberty, which have ever since been asserted with increasing acceptance.

This principle of individual freedom in religious life . . . was carried over into the struggle for individual freedom in political life which took place in the seventeenth century. The settlement of America . . . was the direct outcome of these fundamental developments in the march of human progress. In the impelling force which brought the Pilgrims to Plymouth, the thought of their religious freedom was predominant. . . . But it is impossible to separate the cause of the great migration in those days from the Puritan movement for a free church and a free government which reached a position of temporary power under Cromwell sufficient to be permanently established under William and Mary.

The cause of all this was a great liberal movement, a revolt against authority imposed from without, and the determination to accept for guidance the light of reason which shines from within.[25]

In setting up Plymouth Colony, the Pilgrims, consistent with the implications of their religious beliefs, established no church. They broke with the dominant pattern of political history, whereby rulers had claimed to be gods or the necessary human mediators between the people and the divine. At Plymouth, rather than one or a few possessing political privileges because of some presumed religious superiority, all had an equal right to political participation.

The Pilgrims lifted "up their eyes to heaven,"[26] and each made the journey later described in *Pilgrim's Progress* a reality in their lives. Every one of them asked Bunyan's question, "What shall I do?" And that question put them on a pilgrimage with a final destination beyond in eternity. Yet, as they passed through this world, these spiritual pilgrims also touched the shores of freedom in this life. Their landing at Plymouth, though but a tiny episode in the grand scheme of things as they saw it, was a landmark in the history of the world.

What Tocqueville termed "the boldest theories of the human mind," all "produced offhand by the originality of men's imaginations," "were proclaimed in the deserts of the New World," "accepted as the future creed of a great people," and "reduced to practice by a community . . .

which had yet brought forth neither generals nor philosophers." [27] Consider this small band of obscure men, putting into practice the principles that would make the reputation of the greatest political sage of the century. They combined the politics of John Locke with the religion of John Bunyan.

Certainly, as Ernest Fortin argues, "Christianity is not in essence a political religion but an altogether different type of religion, . . . one in which the individual's relationship is mediated not by a divine law or one's participation in a covenant that binds a group of people together as members of an earthly community but by faith in the person of Jesus Christ." Yet this direct, individualized, nonpolitical mediation—some would call it the priesthood of believers—has always entailed enormous political implications. Most political orders, including the Roman regime at the time of Christ, have made religious mediational functions their source of authority. The claim of Christ to be the only mediator between God and human beings demolishes all mediational claims of the polity, ancient or modern. Christianity, rejecting all such political presumptions, is therefore inherently revolutionary. Orthodox Christian doctrine, pure of politics and unadulterated by Marxism or other anti-Christian systems, is the true liberation theology.

Professor Fortin states that "the New Testament presupposes the existence of civil society" and assumes that "since Christians were not to form a nation of their own and were not given a law by which such a nation might be governed," Christians "would continue to live under the laws of the particular societies to which they happened to belong." Whether Christians on some occasions might properly engage in revolution will not be discussed here, but another question arises that Professor Fortin does not face. What kind of political order would or should Christians establish when they find themselves, as the Pilgrims did, effectively in a state of nature? Obviously, a regime compatible with Christianity's political implications (liberty, equality, and human rights) would or should be chosen.

III

When Tocqueville visited America in the 1830s, approximately one-third of the inhabitants were descendants of English Puritans who migrated to New England about two hundred years before, in the 1630s. As Tocqueville knew, "Puritanism was not merely a religious doctrine, but corresponded at many points with the most absolute and republican theories."[28] The Puritans who settled Massachusetts Bay Colony brought these political ideas with them, as the writings of their political and religious leaders bear eloquent witness.

Governor John Winthrop succinctly stated several of the most fundamental Puritan political precepts.[29] "Arbitrary government" he defined as "where a people have men set over them, without choice or allowance; who have power to govern them, and judge their causes without a rule . . . God only has this prerogative; whose sovereignty is absolute, and whose will is a perfect rule, and reason itself; so as for man to usurp such authority is tyranny, and impiety. Where the people have liberty to admit or reject their governors, and to require the rule by which they shall be governed and judged, that is not an arbitrary government." Winthrop described the origin of government and the principle of consent in quite Lockean terms: "It is clearly agreed by all, that the care of safety and welfare was the original cause or occasion of many families subjecting themselves to rulers and laws; for no man hath lawful power over another, but by birth or consent, so likewise, by the law of property, no man can have just interest in that which belongs to another, without his consent." In words foreshadowing the Preamble to the United States Constitution, Winthrop gave this definition of a "body politic": "The consent of a certain number of people, to cohabit together, under one government for their safety and welfare."[30]

The Puritan clergy shared these opinions. John Cotton in particular, who found in Scripture and what he called the "light of nature" a basis for government by consent, believed in limited government. In language that reminds us of the *Federalist*, he advocated healthy fear of too much power in too few hands: "Let all the world learn to give to mortal men no greater power than they are content they shall use, for use it they will. . . . It is necessary therefore, that all power that is on earth be limited. . . . It is therefore fit . . . for the People, in whom fundamentally all power lies, to give as much power as God in his word gives to men." Cotton also anticipated the theory of revolution in Locke's *Second Treatise* and the Declaration of Independence. The people and the government have a contract, and if the whole body of the people find that their rulers "have broken the Articles of their Covenant" and violated "the way of justice and happiness, which they have sworn to maintain," "It is . . . lawful to take up arms of defense."[31] Indeed, in

1634 and 1638, the American Revolution in miniature was played out in Massachusetts when Charles I sought to impose full-blown Episcopalianism upon them.[32]

But the American Revolution was fought in the name of the "law of nature and nature's God." Were not the Bay Colony Puritans strictly Bible-and-nothing-but-the-Bible people? By no means. The Puritans were really quite rationalistic. An encyclopedia they frequently used defined the "light of nature" as "the gleam of divine wisdom through which light we perceive the evidentness and firmness of first principles, and of the conclusions depending from them." Samuel Williard, who wrote what was considered a "compleat" systematic theology for his fellow Puritans and "always summarizes New England opinion," defined "the Light of Nature, or Right Reason" as "the Medium by which we are to spell out the Law of Nature" and proclaimed that "all the commands of God are highly rational; and because he treats with men as reasonable creatures, he lays matter of conviction before them, of the reasonableness of their obedience." (With the Puritans, how close we are in some ways even to Arminian Locke's *Reasonableness of Christianity*!) Puritan preacher Increase Mather declared that if ever men did not have the written Word of God, "yet they would know, that such and such things are good, and ought to be done," for everyone has "within him, a candle of the Lord in his own breast." John Cotton maintained that civil customs and political principles spring "from the law of nature, from the rudiments written in the heart." Clergyman John Davenport spoke of "the light and law of nature" and said that "the law of nature is God's law." (How close we are to the Declaration's "laws of nature and nature's God.") William Ames, an English Puritan from whom New England Puritans derived many ideas, stated: "that is not law which is not just and right, and that in morality is called right, which accords with right . . . reason, and right . . . is the law of nature."[33]

Puritan conceptions of right and law were reflected in the written code of laws adopted in 1641. In the Body of Liberties, one of the first documents of its kind, the Bay Colony Puritans took the momentous step of putting specific written limitations on government. Adopting the rhetoric of rights and foreshadowing the many declarations of rights of man and citizen to come in America and the world, the Body of Liberties declared that the liberty of the people must be protected by and from government:

The free fruition of such liberties, immunities and privileges as human-ity, civility, and Christianity call for as due to every man in his place and proportion without impeachment have ever been and ever will be the tran-quility and stability of churches and commonwealths. And the denial or deprival thereof, the disturbance if not the ruin of both.

We hold it therefore our duty and safety whilst we are about further establishing of this government to collect and express all such freedoms as for present we foresee may concern us, and to ratify them with solemn oath.

We do therefore this day religiously and unanimously decree and confirm these following rights, liberties and privileges concerning our churches, and civil state to be respectively impartially and inviolably en-joyed and observed throughout our jurisdiction for ever.[34]

But were not the Bay Colony Puritans persecutors? Yes, they were, and we must confess that "like the beautiful woman in one of Haw-thorne's minor tales, there was just one thing amiss" in the Massachu-setts Puritans.[35] One blemish marred the complexion of New England and the Puritan goal of establishing what Winthrop called a "due form of government both civil and ecclesiastical." One tragic flaw dimmed the shine of the "city on a hill" and doomed the effort to complete the Reformation, the essence of the Puritan mission in Massachusetts.[36]

"The great part of British America," wrote Tocqueville, "was peopled by men who, after having shaken off the authority of the Pope, acknowledged no other religious supremacy." The Puritans' chief ob-jection to the Church of England was that it retained too much resem-blance to the Church of Rome, and they wished to "purify" it of "popery." The settlers of New England therefore brought with them into the New World a form of Christianity that Tocqueville could not "better describe than by styling it democratic and republican religion" that "contributed powerfully to the establishment of a republic and a democracy in public affairs." Thus, said Tocqueville, "from the begin-ning, politics and religion contracted an alliance which has never been dissolved."[37]

The alliance between politics and religion that Tocqueville observed in America in the 1830s, however, differed greatly from the one with which the Massachusetts Puritans began. What Tocqueville saw, para-doxically, rested on a wall of separation between church and state. The alliance the Massachusetts Puritans contracted between politics and re-ligion, however, bridged this wall of separation. In spite of their vehe-

ment opposition to Romanism, they held onto one principle and
practice of the ecclesiastical organization they so despised: the mingling
of church and state. Failing to understand liberty of conscience, the
Bay Colony Puritans held that the church ought to govern the world
and force all, whatever their beliefs, to submit to its power.

Confounding church and state led the Bay Colony Puritans into a
massive contradiction with their basic political principles. Political
rights were restricted to members of approved churches, but "of the
first 20,000 who migrated to Massachusetts during the first decade, less
than 4,000" were in that category.[38] But more than political rights were
lost. Only churches with official government sanction could exist. And
while only a minority of the inhabitants could (or wanted to) qualify
for membership in one of the government churches, everyone was
forced to attend one and to pay the pastors. Government effectively
replaced the Bible as the rule for faith and practice. Laws spelling out
particulars of doctrine placed particular prohibition upon "anabap-
tists" or Baptists, as they were now coming to be known. A law of 1654
made it illegal to oppose infant baptism or even to leave a congregation
while infants were being baptized. Under this law, Baptists were banished from Massachusetts, fined, or whipped. Quakers also came in for
a bad time—some beaten, some banished, some killed.[39]

Puritanism was a continuum: Different Puritans occupied different
places according to their positions on ecclesiastical polity and religious
liberty. Individual Puritans were not always logical, but Puritanism, or
let us say simply Protestantism, had an inner logic. It was the logic of
a single idea—Luther's discovery of the infinite consciousness of "inward religion."[40]

Philosophers may wish to call Protestantism an ideology. But given
the premise (which some understandably may not wish to grant), the
logical conclusion is clear: church and civil democracy and separation
of church and state.

IV

Narrowly escaping capture by English authorities, Thomas Hooker arrived in Massachusetts in 1633. It is reported that soon "after Mr.
Hooker's coming . . . many of the freemen grew to be jealous of their
liberties."[41] Within three years of his arrival, Hooker had moved south
and founded the colony of Connecticut, where he began articulating

political views distinctively more democratic than those of the Bay Colony leadership, who in practice were quite oligarchical.[42]

In an exchange by letter with John Winthrop, Hooker disagreed with the latter's opinion regarding "the unwarrantableness and unsafeness of referring matters of counsel or judicature to the body of the people." Winthrop believed that "the best part is always the least, and of that best part the wiser part is always the lesser." Hooker agreed that usually the people should not rule directly—that "the people should choose some amongst them" to rule and "refer matter of counsel to their counselors, matter of judicature to their judges." But still unanswered was "what rule the judge must have to judge by," and "who those counselors were to be." Strongly arguing for the rule of law, Hooker regarded "as a way which leads straight to tyranny" the notion that "in the matter which is referred to the judge the sentence should lie in his breast, or be left to his discretion." Hooker based his case for the rule of law on both Old and New Testament (Deut. 17:10–11, Acts) but also cited Aristotle: "You well know what the heathen man said by the light of common sense: The law is not subject to passion, not to be taken aside with self seeking ends, and therefore ought to have chief rule over rulers themselves." As for who ought to be consulted as counselors in the making of decisions, Hooker argued that "in matters of greater consequence, which concern the common good, a general counsel chosen by all to transact business which concerns all . . . [is] most suitable to rule and most safe."[43]

Hooker was primarily a preacher and a pastor, not a political philosopher. But his depth in matters of divinity caused him to probe for first principles that carried implications for civil government. In his work *The Summe of Church-Discipline*, for example, Hooker developed the concept of church covenants, but he did so by analyzing covenants in general. Hooker's reasoning on covenants or contracts and the principle of consent so closely resembles that of Locke that one historian has remarked, "Hooker could have written Chapters 7 and 8 of Locke's *Second Treatise*."[44] Hooker proclaimed that "in all covenants betwixt Prince and People, Husband and Wife, Master and Servant," and "in all confederations and corporations, there must of necessity be a mutual engagement, each of the other, by their free consent, before any by any rule of God they have any right or power, or can exercise either, each towards the other." Hooker well knew that as matter of history, few civil societies actually originated from an express act of consent; he thus allowed for what he called an "Implicit Covenant," virtually identical to Locke's "tacit consent."[45] As the principle of legitimacy, however, Hooker insisted upon "the free consent of the people." This he repeated in his famous election sermon of May 31, 1638. Taking as his text Deuteronomy 1:13, Hooker laid down as doctrine that "the choice of public magistrates belongs unto the people, by God's own allowance."[46]

The hand of Hooker is clearly evident in the Fundamental Orders of Connecticut, the plan of government for the new colony adopted on January 14, 1639. Considered the "first in the series of written constitutions framed by the people for the people,"[47] and lying in a path of development leading straight to the Constitution of the United States as well as to the constitutions of the separate states after independence, the Fundamental Orders adopted for the colony served as the frame of government even after Connecticut became a state. In 1835 historian George Bancroft could write of the Fundamental Orders: "More than two centuries have elapsed; the world has been made wiser by the most various experience; political institutions have become the theme on which the most powerful and cultivated minds have been employed, and so many constitutions have been framed or reformed, stifled or subverted, that memory may despair of a complete catalogue: but the people of Connecticut have found no reason to deviate essentially from the frame of government established by their fathers. Equal laws were the basis of their commonwealth; and therefore its foundations were lasting." In keeping with Hooker's teachings, the preamble of the Fundamental Orders was an express social contract, an "Explicit Covenant." In eleven short articles, the Orders spelled out the specific institutions and powers of the government, which was a representative democracy. In the government established, "All power was to proceed from the people."[48]

Under Hooker's leadership, Connecticut took a giant step down the road of political freedom. There was an established church, but citizens did not have to be members to qualify as freemen with voting rights. With this extension of the franchise, Connecticut remained much more consistent with the principle of consent than the Bay Colony did. From Hooker's remarkable sermon in which he announced that "the foundation of authority is laid, firstly, in the free consent of the people," observed President Coolidge, "history saw at once that doctrine completely recognized and established, in the free republic under a written constitution, of the Colony of Connecticut. Such was the first offspring of the Puritan spirit of Massachusetts. It was possessed of a vitality capable of creating a political structure of great strength and forming free institutions wherever it might go."[49] It remained for another Puritan and another offspring of Massachusetts to go all the way down the road of religious and civil liberty.

V

In the speeches and deeds of Roger Williams, we witness the transformation of the original Puritan mission of building a "city on a hill" into America's national vision of itself as a land of complete religious and civil liberty. He reached far into the future of America. And though Puritans became his near deadly enemy, we must not forget that Williams was himself a Puritan and based all his thought and action on the first principles of evangelical religion. Roger Williams is wrongly claimed as a kind of patron saint of the ACLU. Instead, he favored separation of church and state for religious reasons—as the position compatible with true Christianity as he understood it.

Williams immigrated to Massachusetts in 1631 but by 1635 had been banished for holding certain "divers new and dangerous opinions." He had reached the conclusion "that the magistrate might not punish . . . a breach of the first table" of the Decalogue.[50] Carrying the Puritan principle of inward religion to its logical conclusion, Williams believed that true religion—the only kind of religion that could possibly save a person—is a free heart belief, what Locke would call in his *Letter concerning Toleration* an "inward persuasion of the mind."[51] Obviously government cannot produce that kind of religion and should not try to do the impossible. Believing in "soul liberty" and drawing the ultimate Puritan conclusion, Williams favored absolute church-state separation and unfettered exercise of religion. From Rhode Island, this "prophet in a wilderness" preached his doctrines to the world.[52]

Roger Williams wrote his most famous work, *The Bloody Tenet of Persecution for Cause of Conscience*, while in England seeking a charter for his newly founded colony. In the aftermath of the Great Civil War and the Puritan Revolution, England was in great turmoil over politics and religion. A personal friend of Oliver Cromwell and John Milton, both of whom leaned toward the more advanced wing of Puritanism in

matters of republican politics and religious freedom, Williams intended
The Bloody Tenet for his Puritan brethren on both sides of the Atlantic.

In his political thought, Williams began with a religious premise:
"civil government is an ordinance of God, to conserve the civil peace of
people, so far as concerns their bodies and goods."[53] He concluded that
"the sovereign, original and foundation of civil power lies in the
people," who "may erect and establish what form of government seems
to them most convenient for their condition." Such governments have
no more power, and for no longer a time, than "the people consenting
and agreeing shall betrust them with." Williams considered this "clear
not only in reason, but in the experience of all commonwealths": "All
lawful magistrates in the world, both before the coming of Christ Jesus,
and since, (excepting those unparalleled typical magistrates of the
Church of Israel) are but derivatives and agents immediately derived
and employed as eyes and hands, serving for the good of the whole:
Hence they have and can have no more power than fundamentally lies
in the bodies or fountains themselves, which power, might, or authority, is not religious, Christian, etc., but natural, humane and civil."

In the principle of consent, of course, Williams differed scarcely at
all from most other Puritans, even those of Massachusetts Bay. But
because he departed from them so greatly on church–state separation
and religious liberty, he (and his cofounders of Rhode Island) could be
more precise and consistent in application. The key matter over which
Williams broke with the Puritans of the Bay Colony was "that commonly received and not questioned opinion, viz. that the civil state and
the spiritual, the church and commonwealth, they are like Hippocrates'
twins, they are born together, grow up together, laugh together, weep
together, sicken and die together." Williams believed that opinion to be
absolutely wrong and contrary to Christianity, and his very first point
in *The Bloody Tenet* was this: "First, that the blood of so many hundred
thousand souls of Protestants and Papists, spilt in the wars of present
and former ages, for their respective conscience, is not required nor
accepted by Jesus Christ the Prince of Peace." Williams considered toleration and separation of church and state to be the correct Christian
position: "It is the will and command of God that (since the coming of
his Son the Lord Jesus) a permission of the most paganish, Jewish,
Turkish, or Antichristian consciences and worships, be granted to all
men in all nations and countries: and they are only to be fought against
with that sword which is only (in soul matters) able to conquer, to wit,
the sword of God's spirit, the Word of God. An enforced uniformity of

religion throughout a nation or civil state, confounds the civil and religious, denies the principles of Christianity and civility, and that Jesus
Christ is come in the Flesh." It is as if Williams wrote with Locke's
Letter concerning Toleration open at his side—or perhaps the other way
around!—so closely does Williams's thesis resemble Locke's first premise: Toleration is so agreeable to the gospel of Jesus Christ and to common reason that "I esteem that to be the chief characteristic mark of
the true church."[54]

Williams contended that merger of church and state promotes neither civil peace nor Christianity. God does not require "uniformity of
religion to be enacted and enforced in any civil state," for sooner or
later it "is the greatest occasion of civil war, ravishing of conscience,
persecution of Christ Jesus in his servants, and of the hypocrisy and
destruction of millions of souls." Only toleration "can procure a firm
and lasting peace"; "true civility and Christianity may both flourish
. . . notwithstanding the permission of divers and contrary consciences, either of Jew or gentile." It is commonly said that whereas
Jefferson advocated separation of church and state from the point of
view of the state and civil peace, Roger Williams did so from the point
of view of the church and correct doctrine. Whatever may be true of
Jefferson, it is clear that Williams proposed a wall of separation between church and state for the sake of both.

On the one hand, argued Williams, the state should leave the
churches alone, for the authority of states extends "no further than over
the bodies or goods of their subjects, not over their souls, and therefore
. . . may not undertake to give laws unto the souls or consciences of
men." He specifically ruled out any right of civil government to tax for
the support of churches:

> It is reasonable to expect and demand of such as live within the state a
> civil maintenance of their civil officers, and to force it where it is denied.
> It is reasonable for a school-master to demand his recompence for his
> labor in his school: but is not reasonable to expect or force it from stran-
> gers, enemies, rebels to that city, from such as come not within, or else
> would not be received into the school. What is the church of Jesus Christ,
> but the city, the school, and family of Christ? The officers of this city,
> school, family, may reasonably expect maintenance from such they min-
> ister unto, but not from strangers, enemies, etc.

On the other hand, churches must never resort to political means
and methods: "The church of Christ doth not use the arm of secular

power to compel men to the true profession of the truth, for this is to
be done with spiritual weapons, whereby Christians are to be exhorted,
not compelled." From the separation of church and state, Williams expected Christianity to grow in strength. While "there is no doctrine, no
tenet so directly tending to break" civil peace than the "doctrine of
persecuting or punishing each other for the cause of conscience or religion," at the same time "the free permitting of the consciences and
meetings of conscionable and faithful people throughout the nation,
and the free permission of the nation to frequent such assemblies, will
be one of the principal means . . . for the propagating and spreading
of the Gospel of the Son of God."

Roger Williams had ideals, but he was no mere idealist. He had vision but was no mere visionary. This was no airy, romantic, purely
theoretical thinker but a man of action who lived a full life and put his
ideals, vision, and theory into practice. A statue of Williams stands in
the Capitol, but his true monument is Rhode Island, which more than
any other colony embodied the principles of the future nation, a "free
church in a free state." Had Rhode Island been larger, "the world
would have been filled with wonder and admiration at the phenomena
of its history."[55] The government established was "Democratical: that
is to say, a Government held by the free and voluntary consent of all,
or the greater part of the free Inhabitants."[56] There was no religious
qualification for political rights and no established church.

Williams desired that the colony "might be for a shelter for persons
distressed for conscience." Others fled to this asylum from religious
persecution—many, such as Quakers, with whom Williams could not
agree in fundamentals of religion and many, most notably Baptists,
with whom he found much to agree (he was for a period a practicing
Baptist) and who played a major role in the development of Rhode
Island (Baptist John Clark is considered cofounder with Williams). In
the history of persecution, Baptists have possibly suffered more at the
hands of "Christians" than have any other group except the Jews.

In 1684, responding to an inquiry from Jews who asked if they might
find a home in the colony, the people of Rhode Island said: "We declare
that they may expect as good protection here as any stranger, not being
of our nation residing among us, ought to have." Thus it came about
that "in August, 1684, the Jews, who from the time of their expulsion
from Spain had had no safe resting place, entered the harbor of Newport to find equal protection, and in a few years to build a house of

God for a Jewish congregation."[57] Their descendants were the "Hebrew Congregation in Newport" to whom Washington wrote his letter of 1790: "May the children of the stock of Abraham, who dwell in this land, continue to merit and enjoy the good will of the other inhabitants while every one shall sit in safety under his own vine and fig tree, and there shall be none to make him afraid."[58]

When Martin Luther stood before the Diet of Worms in 1521 and refused to recant against his conscience, he spoke not only for himself but for all men and women. His claim of conscience is one that all people may make, and it was at the bottom of the Protestant Reformation. The Puritans who settled Massachusetts came here to live as fully in accordance with the principles of the Reformation as they could. But the credit for having succeeded in the Puritans' own goals must go to others—to those who could see that only a society that legally recognizes the claims of conscience may truly say it has completed the Reformation. Rhode Island was the true city on a hill of colonial America, a prophetic microcosm, forerunner of a nation that would be a beacon of civilization to the modern world.

VI

What made it self-evident to the generation of the founders that men are equal and possess rights to life, liberty, and the pursuit of happiness? A self-evident truth "is not one which everyone necessarily admits to be true." Two plus two equals four will remain true even if everyone in the world denies it. A self-evident truth "is one the evidence for which is contained in the terms of the proposition, and which is admitted to be true by everyone who already grasps the meaning of the terms." The doctrine of natural equality and rights in the Declaration of Independence is therefore inextricably bound up with the presumed "specific nature of man and . . . its difference from other species."[59]

For the founding generation, human equality and rights were logically entailed in the phrase "all men," but not so much arid abstraction as fervent faith moved their minds. Burke claimed, "The little catechism of the rights of man is soon learned; and the inferences are in the passions," to which Strauss added, "What is required to make modern natural right effective is enlightenment or propaganda rather than moral appeal."[60] However true that may be for Hobbesian natural

right, it misrepresents the psychological—not to say philosophical—
basis for the rights of man in the Puritan/Protestant version. The conclusions may well be in the passions, if we consider moral indignation
among them; but the premises are in the convictions—moral and religious ones. And what is required to make this "modern natural right"
effective is neither enlightenment nor propaganda but preaching.

Generally, the clergy of colonial America did not speak about politics. But there were exceptions, and one of those occasions in New
England was the Annual Election Sermon in which preachers reminded
people of their duty to civil government and, as the primary political
teachers of the people, instructed the common person in political fundamentals.

After Locke's *Second Treatise* became so widely read in America,
preachers frequently quoted it on those few occasions when they
deemed it proper to speak of politics. These preachers, especially those
in New England, often spoke in Lockean language of the laws of nature
and nature's God. But the basic content of such preaching was nothing
new. "It was hardly accidental," as one historian points out, "that New
England ministers gave the first and most cordial reception to the arguments of John Locke . . . and broadcast from their pulpits . . . government by consent."[61] The Puritans had been preaching such views
for about a half-century.

What of the more philosophically tutored elite—the founding fathers
themselves? We ought not overestimate the superiority of their education over that of the preachers of the day. Neither should we forget that
the "Lockean consensus" was as much taken for granted by them as it
was by the people. After all, the *Federalist*, as close as our fathers came
to original political philosophy, is no discourse about the meaning of
justice; their dialogue with the anti-Federalists was mostly about
means, not ends. The Declaration of Independence, containing the
"harmonizing sentiments of the day," is a monument to the political
wisdom of the people. The fathers have their memorial in the compar-
atively pedestrian work of the Constitution, more a feat of political
engineering than of political philosophizing or theologizing.

But we ought not create too great a gulf between the people of that
generation and their leaders. It seems a mistake to read any significance
into the fact that the founders frequently called God by other names
(e.g., "Divine Parent," "Supreme Being"). From the standpoint of orthodoxy, the worst that can be charged against the founders is deism;

yet deism is still a kind of theism and not atheism. That does not render their political principles per se nonreligious.

Perhaps they did believe only in the "god of the philosophers." But that divinity in modernity is a being far different from his counterpart among the ancients. The latter was no creator and no lawgiver, as the God of Newton and Locke and Jefferson most certainly was. Not all philosophers' gods are created equal.

Some note that reason cannot refute special revelation, and special revelation cannot refute reason, but special revelation sustains a much more positive relation to reason or "natural revelation" than that. The Bible, special revelation, vouches for natural revelation, declaring that it should be obvious to human reason that God is creator: "Because that which may be known of God is manifest in them; for God hath shown it unto them. For the invisible things of him from the creation of the world are clearly seen, being understood by the things that are made, even his eternal power and Godhead, so that they are without excuse" (Romans 1:19–20). Yet the Bible also teaches that this same obvious (self-evident?) truth is one that people inherently reject, changing the truth for a lie, professing themselves to be wise, and becoming fools who say there is no God. It seems that human beings need the special revelation to see the natural revelation, especially in that part of nature most close to home—themselves. In the language of philosophy:

The recognition of the identity of the Subject and God was introduced into the world when *the fullness of Time was come;* the consciousness of this identity is the recognition of God in his true essence. . . . The nature of God as pure Spirit, is manifested to man *in the Christian religion.*

But what is Spirit? It is the one immutably homogeneous Infinite— pure Identity—which in its second phase separates itself from itself and makes this second aspect its own polar opposite. . . . If Spirit be defined as absolute reflection within itself in virtue of its absolute duality . . . it is recognized as *Triune:* the "Father" and the "Son," and that duality which essentially characterizes it as "Spirit." . . . *in* this truth, the relation of man *to* this truth is also posited. For Spirit makes itself its own oppo- site—and is the return from this opposite into itself. . . . That antithetic form of Spirit is the Son of God . . . the unity of Man with God is posited in the Christian Religion. But this unity must not be superficially con- ceived, as if God were only Man, and Man, without further condition, were God . . . implicit unity exists in the first place only for the thinking speculative consciousness; but it must also exist for the sensuous, representative consciousness—it must become an object for the World—it must *appear*, and that in the sensuous form appropriate to Spirit, which is the human. *Christ has appeared*—a Man who is God—God who is Man; and thereby peace and reconciliation have accrued to the World.[62]

Certainly American political thought of the Revolutionary era was imbued with the ideas described by John Locke in the *Second Treatise*. In its most important passages, the Declaration of Independence reads like a paraphrase of Locke. Scholars correctly speak of the "Lockean consensus" in eighteenth-century America, meaning the near-universal agreement on the principles of the *Second Treatise*, which was, indeed, the political science textbook for the age. However, it is no detraction from "the esteemed Locke," as admiring Americans referred to him, to point out that long before he wrote the *Second Treatise*, our Pilgrim and Puritan forebears, employing their common-sense reasonings, discovered the same moral maxims and political principles. The Declaration of Independence expressed the common sense of a most uncommon people. For eighteenth-century Americans, Locke was a voice of human reason—and a very prestigious one—confirming what they already believed. Inquiry, in the spirit of Socrates, ought to begin with and give due credit to the "common sense" of that most uncommon people, the true authors of the Declaration of Independence.

Infinitely more important than the role of Locke's book in eighteenth-century America was the role of the Book of Books. The rock-bottom consensus in colonial America was a biblical consensus. Not all Americans were Christian converts; many—some among the founders—had heard the Christian gospel and explicitly rejected it. But there were few Americans who had not heard the Bible preached and had their thinking deeply influenced, even if in ways not consciously realized.

President Coolidge was right: "No one can escape the conclusion that in the great outline of its principles the Declaration was the result of the religious teachings of the preceding period." These teachers "preached equality because they believed in the fatherhood of God and the brotherhood of men" and "justified freedom by the text that we are all created in the divine spirit."[63] The secularists of the left who would strip all religious meaning from the public sector and in the name of separation of church and state erect a wall between God and government speak and act in the name of democracy. In reality, they destroy the original foundation for democracy in America.

Liberal democracy faces a crisis of belief. It is too late for philosophy to help by "giving instruction as to what the world ought to be"; "philosophy . . . always comes on the scene too late to give it." Plato could do nothing to arrest the decline of his day. Certainly a contemporary Platonic political philosophy that claims to defend natural right but at best offers noble lies, at worst offers nihilism and atheism, can give no aid. Even in Plato's day "aid had to come from on High," and so it must in our own.[64] "Equality, liberty, popular sovereignty, the rights of man," declared President Coolidge, "these are not elements which we can see and touch. They are ideals. They have their source and their roots in the religious convictions. They belong in the unseen world. Unless the faith of the American people in these religious convictions is to endure, the principles of our Declaration will perish. We can not continue to enjoy the result if we neglect and abandon the cause."[65] Perhaps we may call "supply-side religion" the theory that there is nothing government can or should do to help promote that true and saving religion which is an inward persuasion of the mind. Werner Dannhauser has noted that the founding fathers "surely opposed frontal assault on the fund of faith bequeathed to them by puritanism, though our hindsight makes us wonder whether they were concerned enough about its depletion." But he seems to imply that the fact that they made no provision for governmental support of religion demonstrates insufficient concern for faith. To the contrary, they—and the massive numbers of evangelical Christians who were among the main supporters of the First Amendment—believed that religious liberty and church-state separation fostered real faith. That was the view held by so many to whom Tocqueville talked,[66] and the spectacular Christian expansion in the nineteenth century under the new regime of freedom provides striking evidence for the correctness of that position.[67]

Conservative philosophers attracted to ecclesiastical establishment as the remedy for society's religious support for morality should be reminded that they thereby sign death warrants for many, perhaps even for themselves. Neither do they do anything to help liberal democracy. Better that they should pray. As one wise man said:

> While . . . the correct sentiment is adopted, that the State is based on Religion, the position thus assigned to religion supposes the State already to exist; and that subsequently, in order to maintain it, Religion must be brought into it—in buckets and bushels as it were—and impressed upon people's hearts.

If that outcry—that urging and striving for the implantation of Religion in the community—were an utterance of anguish and a call for help . . . expressing the danger of religion having vanished, or being about to vanish entirely from the State—that would be fearful indeed—worse, in fact, than this outcry supposes: for it implies the belief in a resource against the evil, viz., the implantation and inculcation of religion; whereas religion is by no means a thing to be so produced; its *self-production* (and there can be no other) lies much deeper.[68]

Notes

1. Leo Strauss, *Natural Right and History* (Chicago: University of Chicago Press, 1953), pp. 1–2.

2. Thomas Landon Thorson, *The Logic of Democracy* (New York: Holt, Rinehart and Winston, 1962), p. 141.

3. See Jude Wanniski, *The Way the World Works* (New York: Simon and Schuster Touchstone Books, 1978), pp. 120–22; also Jack Kemp, *An American Renaissance: A Strategy for the Eighties* (New York: Harper & Row, 1978), p. 59. Also see a provocative study, Thomas B. Silver, "Coolidge and the Historians," *American Scholar* 50 (Autumn 1981): 501–17.

4. Calvin Coolidge, "The Inspiration of the Declaration," in *Foundations of the Republic* (New York: Books for Libraries Press, 1968), pp. 450–51.

5. Strauss, *Natural Right and History*, p. 7.

6. Ibid., p. 166.

7. Coolidge, "The Inspiration of the Declaration," p. 454.

8. Alexis de Tocqueville, *Democracy in America*, vol. 1, ed. Philips Bradley (New York: Alfred A. Knopf, 1963), pp. 26, 28, 30–31.

9. Quoted in C. J. Friedrich, "Introduction to Dover Edition," G. W. F. Hegel, *The Philosophy of History*, trans. J. Sibvee (New York: Dover, 1956).

10. George Bancroft, *History of the United States of America*, vol. 1 (Boston: Little, Brown, and Company, 1879), pp. 210–11.

11. Quoted in Walter H. Burgess, *John Robinson, Pastor of the Pilgrim Fathers: A Study of His Life and Times* (New York: Harcourt, Brace & Howe, 1920), p. 117.

12. John Locke, *Second Treatise of Government*, ed. Thomas Peardon (Indianapolis: Bobbs-Merrill, 1952), pp. 4, 13.

13. See ibid., chap. 5, "Of Property," sec. 34.

14. The words of William Bradford, Pilgrim political leader whose *History of Plymouth Plantation* became the first American history book; see *Bradford's History of Plymouth Plantation, 1606–1646*, ed. William T. Davis (New York: Barnes and Noble, Inc. 1908), p. 106.

15. Locke, *Second Treatise*, p. 54.

16. Winston Churchill, *History of the English-Speaking Peoples: The New World* (New York: Dodd, Mead & Company), p. 170.

17. "The Mayflower Compact," *The Primary Sources of American Government*, ed. Randall H. Nelson and John J. Wuest (New York: G. P. Putnam's Sons, 1962), p. 10.

18. Calvin Coolidge, "Massachusetts and the Nation," *The Price of Freedom* (New York: Charles Scribner's Sons, 1974), p. 249.

19. Quoted in Francis Bradley, *The American Proposition: A New Type of Man* (New York: Moral Re-armament, 1977), pp. 110–11; see also Jerry H. Combee and Cline E. Hall, "The Pilgrims," *Evangelical Beacon*, Nov. 15, 1982, pp. 4–5.

20. Bancroft, *History of the U.S.*, p. 244.

21. Samuel Eliot Morison, *The Story of the "Old Colony" of New Plymouth* (New York: Alfred A. Knopf, 1956), p. 152.

22. Bancroft, *History of the U.S.*, p. 244.

23. John S. Barry, "English Pilgrims Settle at Plymouth," in *The Great Events by Famous Historians*, vol. 11 (New York: The National Alumni, 1905), p. 109.

24. Jean-Jacques Rousseau, *The Social Contract*, in *Social Contract: Essays by Locke, Hume, and Rousseau*, ed. Ernest Barker (New York: Oxford University Press, 1962), p. 304.

25. Coolidge, "Massachusetts and the Nation," p. 247–51.

26. *Bradford's History of Plymouth Plantation*, p. 79.

27. Tocqueville, *Democracy in America*, p. 42.

28. Ibid.

29. See the discussion of Puritan political ideas in Perry Miller, *The New England Mind: The Seventeenth Century* (Boston: Beacon Press, 1961), chap. 14, "The Social Covenant."

30. John Winthrop, "A Defense of the Order of the Court Made in the Year 1637," in *Political Thought in America*, ed. Andrew M. Scott (New York: Rinehart and Company, 1959), p. 17. Of course, Winthrop and his fellow Puritans did not always practice what they preached; but see Miller, *New England Mind*, p. 409: "That magistrates were limited by the compact, that government should be by laws and not by men, that the covenant was annulled by any serious violation of the terms, and that the people possessed a right to resist all such infringements—these principles were declared no less emphatically in Puritan theory than in the Declaration of Independence. The so-called theocracies of New England never lost sight of them, and whenever their own deeds were called in question they endeavored, after the example of John Winthrop, to exonerate themselves according to the first principles of contractualism."

31. Quoted in Miller, *New England Mind*, pp. 409–10. "John Cotton put the case for

the limitation of rulers as bluntly as any radical of the eighteenth century" (p. 409).

32. See Bancroft, *History of the U.S.*, pp. 323–28.

33. Miller, *New England Mind*, pp. 199, 185–86, 197–98.

34. See the excerpts in *Political Thought in America*, pp. 12–16.

35. Adapted from Melville's *Billy Budd*.

36. See Miller, *New England Mind*, pp. 463–71.

37. Tocqueville, *Democracy in America*, p. 300.

38. E. E. Rich, "The European Nations and the Atlantic," in *The New Cambridge Modern History*, vol. 4, ed. J. P. Cooper (Cambridge: Cambridge University Press, 1971), p. 686.

39. A total of four Quakers were put to death in Massachusetts.

40. See the preface to Hegel's *The Philosophy of Right*, trans. T. M. Knox, in *Great Books of the Western World*, vol. 46, ed. R. M. Hutchins (Chicago: Encyclopedia Britannica, 1952), p. 7.

41. William Hubbard (1621–1704), New England Puritan historian, quoted in Clinton Rossiter, *Seedtime of the Republic: The Origin of the American Tradition of Political Liberty* (New York: Harcourt, Brace and Company, 1953), p. 164.

42. See Curtis P. Nettels, *The Roots of American Civilization*, 2d ed. (New York: Appleton-Century-Crofts, 1963), p. 170.

43. Rossiter, *Seedtime of the Republic*, pp. 170–171.

44. Ibid., p. 172.

45. Locke, *Second Treatise*, p. 68.

46. The full outline of Hooker's sermon is in Rossiter, *Seedtime of the Republic*, p. 171.

47. Bancroft, *History of the U.S.*, p. 318. However, some would extend the honor of being the first written American Constitution to the Plymouth Pilgrims' General Fundamentals of 1636.

48. Ibid., p. 319.

49. Coolidge, "Massachusetts and the Nation," pp. 254–55.

50. Rossiter, *Seedtime of the Republic*, pp. 181–82.

51. John Locke, *A Letter concerning Toleration*, with an introduction by Patrick Romanell (Indianapolis: Bobbs-Merrill, 1959), p. 18.

52. As described in Perry Miller, *Roger Williams: His Contribution to the American Tradition* (Indianapolis: Bobbs-Merrill, 1953), p. 49.

53. Selections from Roger Williams's writings may be found in *Political Thought in America*, pp. 21–29, and Miller, *Roger Williams*.

54. Locke, *Letter concerning Toleration*, p. 13.

55. Bancroft, *History of the U.S.*, p. 301.

56. Rossiter, *Seedtime of the Republic*, p. 190.

57. Bancroft, *History of the U.S.*, p. 431.

58. Quoted in Paul F. Boller, Jr., *George Washington and Religion* (Dallas: Southern Methodist University Press, 1963), p. 186.

59. Harry V. Jaffa, "On the Nature of Civil and Religious Liberty," in *The Conservative Papers*, ed. Ralph de Toledano and Karl Hess (New York: Doubleday Anchor, 1964), pp. 250–68, quoted in *American Conservative Thought in the Twentieth Century*, ed. William F. Buckley (Indianapolis: Bobbs-Merrill, 1970), p. 228.

60. Strauss, *Natural Right and History*, p. 183.

61. Rossiter, *Seedtime of the Republic*, p. 53.

62. Hegel, *Philosophy of History*, pp. 323–26.

63. Coolidge, "The Inspiration of the Declaration," pp. 450–51.

64. Hegel, *The Philosophy of Right*, pp. 5, 7; see also S. B. Drury, "The Esoteric Philosophy of Leo Strauss," *Political Theory* 13 (August 1985): 315–37, and T. L. Pangel, ed., *Studies in Platonic Political Philosophy* (Chicago: University of Chicago Press, 1983).

65. Coolidge, "The Inspiration of the Declaration," p. 451.

66. Tocqueville, *Democracy in America*, p. 308.

67. For a brief discussion of this phenomenon and its significance, see Jerry Combee and Cline Hall, *Designed for Destiny* (Wheaton, Ill.: Tyndale, 1985), esp. pp. 57–58.

68. Hegel, *Philosophy of History*, pp. 51–52.

Socrates' Understanding of the Problem of Religion and Politics

PETER AHRENSDORF

In recent years the issue of religion and politics, or the question of the proper relation between religion and political society, has emerged as one of the most hotly debated issues in America. Supporters of a greater political role for religion warn that the growing secularization of America frustrates the religious yearnings of our citizens and threatens our society with moral decline. Their opponents express the fear that a revival of religion in the political arena will lead to the intimidation and, eventually, persecution of religious and nonreligious minorities. The current debate has taken place within the framework of our principles of the separation of church and state and of the freedom of religion, principles reflected in our Constitution. But our Constitution's provisions dealing with religion and politics were themselves decisively influenced by the early modern political philosophers' understanding of the proper relation between religion and political society. In order, then, to understand the theoretical framework of the current debate about religion and politics, it seems reasonable to examine those political philosophers' treatment of this problem.

Generally speaking, the early modern political philosophers whose teachings played a decisive role in the founding of our regime—Hobbes, Spinoza, and Locke—regarded the political power of religion as harmful to political society. In their view, established religion tends to foster civil strife and persecution. Consequently, they sought to weaken the political authority of religion either by separating the church from the state or by subordinating the church to the state's authority. But these political philosophers did not believe that such a political reform alone would put an end to the ills that religion fostered. They understood that as long as religious passions remained strong in men's souls—such passions as the longing for salvation and the fear of damnation—religious wars and the oppression of religious and nonreligious minorities were likely to persist. Accordingly, they sought not only to weaken the institutional power of religion over political society but also to attenuate the religious passions within each member of society. Their political reform of society required a psychological reform of man. They proposed a society in which religious authority was to be subordinated to political authority, a multiplicity of religious sects was to be tolerated, and men were to be encouraged to pursue their enlightened self-interest, that is, their worldly political and economic interests. It was their hope that in such a liberal and commercial society, peace and prosperity would command more of people's interest and energies than heaven and hell, and hence that human beings would escape from the ills of religious strife and religious persecution.

These political philosophers did not, however, understand the problem of religion and politics solely in terms of the proper relation between religion and political society. In their view there was a third component of the problem: political philosophy itself. The political and psychological power of religion was harmful not only to political society, they believed, but also to political philosophers. For since the execution of Socrates, the founder of political philosophy, for impiety, political philosophers had suffered from religious persecution. The activity of political philosophy—namely, the rational inquiry into the proper ends of political society—had always brought political philosophers into conflict with the priests, who claimed to know the proper ends of political society from God or from the gods. Political philosophers of all ages, then, have sought to understand not only the proper relation between religion and political society but also the proper relation between them both and political philosophy. They understood the issue to be: Whose influence should prevail in the political community, that of the priests or that of the philosophers, that of religion or that of reason?

Hobbes, Spinoza, and Locke argued that their influence should prevail over that of the priests. Their argument was based on the claim that there is a certain commonality of interest between political philosophers and society as a whole. Both had suffered from religious persecution and religious strife. And both would benefit from the establishment of liberal, commercial societies enlightened by the teachings of political philosophy. Such societies would be good because they would promote the peace and prosperity of society as a whole, and because they would protect political philosophy from religious persecution and liberate it from religious supervision.

A liberal, commercial society, then, such as we have in this country, constitutes the modern political philosophers' solution to the problem of religion, politics, and philosophy. Yet the recent outcry against the secularization of our society suggests that a significant number of our citizens are dissatisfied with the condition of religion in America today. And the increasing involvement of religious groups in political causes of all kinds suggests that there is an increasing willingness to accept the subordination of religious authority to the secular political authorities. In less visible forms, a certain longing for religion may be detected in our intellectual circles as well. There is much discussion in universities of the longing for "the sacred." Artists' attempts to found a religion of art bespeak a belief that some kind of religion is necessary for society. And even the often-heard denunciations of American materialism may spring from displaced religious longings that cannot be satisfied in liberal or, for that matter, Communist societies.

It is possible that we are witnessing the reawakening of religious yearnings, if not religious belief, in America today. Such a reawakening would not be altogether surprising. For a century and a half ago, Tocqueville described Americans as a very religious people. Today, Americans seem markedly less religious. But the question arises, have the religious passions the Americans had in Tocqueville's time vanished, or are they merely dormant? And if they are dormant, might they reawaken in new and dangerous forms? Can strong religious passions be satisfied in a society such as ours? Such questions should lead us to wonder, at least, about the early modern political philosophers' claim to have solved the problem of religion, politics, and philosophy. Moreover, those philosophers' proposed solution to this problem constituted an explicit rejection of their premodern predecessors' understanding of the proper relation among religion, political society, and philosophy. Insofar as we have come to doubt the success of the modern solution to this problem, it seems reasonable to examine the alternative understanding of this problem presented by older political philosophers.

Although Socrates was executed by Athens for impiety, he did not anticipate the early modern political philosophers by proposing the formation of a liberal society in which philosophers would be protected from religious persecution. He was well aware of the ills that the political power of religion tends to foster, but he seems to have accepted religion as a necessary part of political life. Even in the *Republic*, in which he describes the best regime, he assigns to religion an important role. While Socrates recognized the problematic relation among religion, political society, and philosophy, his understanding of that problem was quite different from that of the early modern philosophers. To discover what Socrates' understanding of that problem was, it is especially useful to study Plato's *Phaedo*. His presentation of Socrates' last conversation before his execution for impiety presents Socrates' analysis of religious impulses. It is on the basis of his psychological analysis of thoses impulses that I believe Socrates would view skeptically the modern philosophers' political reform of society and psychological reform of man.

Plato's *Phaedo* highlights dramatically the problematic relation among religion, politics, and philosophy, for in it the philosopher Socrates is put to death by his city on the grounds that he is impious. The dialogue draws our attention to the grave threat to philosophers posed by the political power of religion. But the *Phaedo* presents more than just the problem of religion, politics, and philosophy as the conflict between the philosopher and the religious political community. For in the conversation that takes place on the day of Socrates' execution, two of his most devoted followers express their disappointment and frustration with philosophy, disappointment and frustration that spring from their own religious yearnings. Socrates goes so far as to compare these students to the Athenians who condemned him to death for impiety. The problem of the religious persecution of philosophers, Socrates suggests, has its roots in the conflict between philosophy and the religious impulses in man, impulses that are so powerful that even admirers of philosophy are moved by them.

The condemnation and execution of Socrates was not an isolated event but rather part of a persistent pattern of religious persecution of philosophers in the Greece of his time. Anaxagoras, Protagoras, and Aristotle all were charged with impiety. According to Plato, the standard charge against philosophers was atheism. In the eyes of the Greek populace, their leaders, and their poets, the philosophers were atheists, and they corrupted the youth by turning them into atheists as well.

The charge of impiety or atheism was an extremely grave charge in the ancient world. Religion was at the core of family and political life in the ancient city. The Greeks claimed to derive their moral codes and their laws from the gods. To call into question the existence of those gods was tantamount to undermining the most fundamental moral rules and the legitimacy of the cities' laws. Consequently, the Greek political communities tended to view the philosophers as peculiarly dangerous criminals and treated them accordingly.

But what was the basis of the widely held opinion that the philosophers were impious? Most simply, the philosophers discovered that the universe is ruled not by gods who reward the righteous and punish the wicked but rather by natural necessities that are indifferent to moral concerns. Eclipses, they discovered, are not signs of the gods' anger but predictable natural phenomena. Thunder and lightning, they taught, are not divine punishments of the wicked but forces of uncaring nature. The philosophers revealed a universe that is deaf to man's demands for cosmic justice. These discoveries shattered the Greeks' vision of a universe that supported and enforced their laws and their moral codes. The philosophers' demystification of the world threatened to delegitimize and demoralize the ancient city. Unwilling or unable to accept this demystification, the cities of ancient Greece strove to quiet and even to silence the philosophers.

The religious persecution of the philosophers threatened to extinguish philosophy altogether in the ancient world. The philosophers were defenseless in the face of the hostility of the Greek cities. The threat of imprisonment, exile, or execution hung over their heads at all times. Over time such persecution must have reduced philosophers to solitude, silence, and, finally, extinction. History bears witness to the success of religious fervor in eradicating what is held to be impious. The most striking example of such success is the fate of philosophy in the Islamic world, where it flourished to an extraordinary degree for two hundred years but subsequently was extinguished by religious fanaticism. At the time of Socrates' execution philosophy was in danger of suffering a similar fate in Greece, the birthplace of philosophy.

The *Phaedo* shows that the religious hostility to philosophy is not confined to the unphilosophic many who have condemned Socrates to death. It emerges, albeit in a gentler form, among the philosophic students of Socrates as well. The principal interlocutors of Socrates in the *Phaedo*, Cebes and Simmias, are two young Thebans who studied philosophy in their native city and then came to Athens to study with

Socrates. We know from the *Crito*, moreover, that Cebes and Simmias were willing to help Socrates escape from prison at considerable risk to themselves. And even after Socrates has spurned their help and refused to escape, they are willing to flaunt the Athenians' judgment that he is a capital criminal by joining him on the day of his execution.

Despite their devotion, Cebes and Simmias express their disappointment with philosophy on two counts: It fails to satisfy both their longing for justice and their desire for perfect wisdom. The condemnation and imminent execution of Socrates offend their sense of justice. The man they admire most is being killed by his enemies. Moreover, they are aware that Socrates' fate is not an isolated one. The unjust execution of Socrates reminds them of the unjust persecution of philosophers in general. Their indignation at this injustice gives rise, however, to a painful feeling of impotence. For these young men do not have the consolation of hoping that Socrates somehow will be rewarded or that his death somehow will be avenged. Cebes and Simmias share the need felt by most people to believe that there is a cosmic support for justice, that there are gods who reward the good and punish the wicked. Indeed, their need to believe in such gods is even greater than that felt by most, for the men they admire most, the philosophers, are especially weak in the face of the hostile political community. As admirers of philosophers they are bound to witness and to suffer from the injustice of persecution. But they are also bound to believe that there is no cosmic support for justice. Only a belief in gods who reward the philosophers and punish their enemies would satisfy their longing for justice, but such a belief, it seems, would require them to reject the teachings of the philosophers. Paradoxically, it is these students' very devotion to the philosophers that inspires in them the desire to believe in gods who are also devoted to the philosophers, yet this desire is at odds with what the philosophers themselves teach about the universe.

These students of Socrates are also disappointed by the failure of philosophy to satisfy their desire for perfect wisdom. Specifically, they complain that no philosopher, including Socrates, has given them clear and certain knowledge about death. The question of death is an important one for Cebes and Simmias, for they know that if they continue to study philosophy they will be endangering their lives. If death brings oblivion to all, it would be reasonable for them to try to prolong their lives at all costs. If death brings rewards to the pious and punishments to the impious, it would be reasonable for them to strive to be as pious as possible even at risk to their lives. But without sure knowledge of death, Cebes and Simmias find themselves fearfully uncertain as to how they should lead their lives. And the execution of Socrates for impiety must heighten their uncertainty, for it reminds them both that the study of philosophy may put their lives in jeopardy and that most men believe that the philosopher is impious and hence that he will be punished in an afterlife. On the day of Socrates' death, Cebes and Simmias are especially eager to know what death holds in store for them in order to determine whether or not they should continue to study philosophy, despite the risks they may run in this life and the next.

The knowledge about death that Cebes and Simmias desire must be clear and certain knowledge. Not only the fear of extinction and the fear of divine punishment but also the fear of uncertainty leads them to desire certain knowledge about death. Throughout the *Phaedo* they exhibit a strong aversion to doubt and perplexity and an impatience to obtain certain answers to the questions that agitate them most. This disposition leads them to be dogmatic, for they are often willing to accept doctrines as certain even when these doctrines are not supported by convincing arguments. For them, wisdom means freedom from doubt through clear and certain knowledge about the most important matters, including death. They had evidently hoped that philosophy would give them such wisdom. But thus far, at least, that hope has gone unfulfilled, and they remain in the grip of painful uncertainty. And since they have a tendency to prefer even specious certainty to honest uncertainty, their disappointment with philosophy may lead them to seek for certainty elsewhere, especially from religion.

The disappointment with philosophy expressed by these students of Socrates is a gentle reflection of the anger with philosophers expressed by the political community as a whole. For the philosophers call into question the authoritative wisdom of the community as it is articulated by the laws, the statesmen, and the poets, without offering any comparably authoritative wisdom in its place. In the *Apology* Socrates says that he exposes the ignorance of Athens's statesmen, poets, and artisans for all to see and then proclaims himself the wisest of men because he alone knows that he is ignorant about the greatest things. But such knowledge of ignorance cannot satisfy the need for certainty about the greatest things felt by most men. Political communities, for example, must claim to know what justice is if they are to command the loyalty of their citizens. Similarly, men must believe they know what death holds in store for them, whether extinction or an afterlife, if they are to be confident that their lives are reasonable and moral. Awareness of one's ignorance about such matters as justice and death is consequently a painful experience for most men, one that fills them with a dizzying perplexity and a chilling fear of the unknown. Accordingly, most men get angry with the philosopher for inflicting this painful experience on them and seek to silence him. For by silencing him they hope to return to the happy state of false certainty they enjoyed before they encountered his troubling questions.

Their disappointment with philosophy for failing to free them from ignorance and uncertainty has not yet led Cebes and Simmias to turn away from philosophy, but there is a great danger that it will in the future. For, according to Socrates, philosophy can never provide them with the perfect wisdom they seek. In his view, human wisdom is necessarily incomplete, since man is necessarily incomplete. For example, because man is mortal he can never have certain knowledge about death. He cannot, strictly speaking, know whether death is oblivion, or whether men are judged by gods in an afterlife. He cannot know for certain whether death is to be feared or to be welcomed. He can know, however, that death is inevitable and that he lacks certain knowledge of what it will bring. And he can also know that human beings, including himself, have a strong passion to possess certain knowledge about death and that this passion leads most men to think they know what death holds in store for them when they don't. Such knowledge about death gives the philosopher a certain wisdom about death, for it frees him from the desperate attachment to life and from the religious terror and hope before death that characterizes most who think they know what death is. The philosopher's knowledge enables him to recognize as false the certitude that men claim to have about death and enables him to examine the passions that lead to such false certitude. And he will be on guard lest he himself be driven by such passions. Moreover, because the philosopher traces religious accounts of an afterlife to longings for cosmic justice and for perfect wisdom, he will doubt that such an afterlife exists. His knowlege of the unknowability of death will lead him to suspect, though not to know for certain, that the religious accounts that purport to teach what death is are false. The philosopher will be inclined neither to cling to life, since he is fully conscious that death is inevitable, nor to welcome or seek death, since he enjoys his life and has little hope for an afterlife. Hence the philosopher alone among human beings learns how to die, for he alone learns how to live with the inevitability and unknowability of death, free from false opinions about death.

More generally, Socratic wisdom means the full awareness of the necessary incompleteness of human knowledge and the ability to live with that awareness. This wisdom is what the famous Socratic formulations reflect: knowledge of our ignorance about the greatest things; learning how to die; knowledge of eros, that is, of our longing for completeness. Such wisdom may be described as theoretical moderation—a continuous, ever-deepening awareness of the necessarily limited character of our knowledge. Socratic wisdom also entails political moderation, for Socrates recognizes that most men cannot live with the awareness of their ignorance. He sees clearly, for example, the unreasonableness of the desires for cosmic justice and for certainty about the most important matters, but he sees with equal clarity that such desires are inextinguishable in most men. Because he believes that there is an unbridgeable gulf between the philosopher and most men, Socrates does not seek to enlighten men as to the unreasonableness of these desires, as modern philosophers sought to do. Instead he accommodates these desires and, when possible, tries to temper them.

Socrates' young companions in the *Phaedo* have not fully recognized the unreasonableness of their desires for justice in the world and for certainty about the greatest things. These passions threaten to drive them away from and even against philosophy, but they are at root religious passions. Socrates teaches that only religion can satisfy the need for certainty about the greatest things—about death, for example—felt by most men. Similarly, only the belief in gods who reward the good and punish the wicked can fully satisfy the human craving for justice. Most human beings, including admirers of philosophy, are moved by such religious impulses. It is not only the political power of religion that threatens philosophy but, more importantly, the religious passions in human souls. And in Socrates' view such passions are enduring features of the human soul. No psychological reform can weaken them or root them out, at least not in the long run. Insofar as the philosopher seeks to protect himself and other philosophers from religious persecution and seeks to educate the young potential philosophers, he must accommodate himself and philosophy to these religious passions. Accordingly, instead of attempting to make society less religious, as Hobbes, Spinoza, and Locke attempt to do, Socrates tries to make philosophy appear, at least, more religious.

Socrates knows that what he says and how he behaves on his dying day will be reported far and wide. The execution of this famous philosopher is bound to inspire curiosity throughout Greece. Moreover, a number of his companions on this day are foreigners, and they will bring news of his last conversation and death to the men in their native cities. Socrates is aware, then, that what he says and does on this day will have a wide and lasting impact on his own reputation and possibly on the overall reputation of philosophy. The circumstances of this conversation give Socrates a unique opportunity to alter the widely held opinion that philosophers are necessarily impious men, and he exploits this opportunity fully.

Plato draws the reader's attention to the breadth of Socrates' audience in the *Phaedo* through the dramatic setting of the dialogue. Instead of presenting Socrates' last conversation and death directly, he presents them through the account that Phaedo, a student of Socrates, gives to other students of philosophy who live far away from Athens. Furthermore, Plato underscores the importance of Phaedo's narration of Socrates' last day by naming the dialogue after him. For the *Phaedo* is the only dialogue that Plato names after the narrator of the dialogue. By repeating his teacher's last conversation to other men, Phaedo fulfills a mission Socrates had entrusted to him: On his last day, Socrates urged Phaedo to do his utmost to keep his philosophic speeches and the activity of philosophic conversation alive after his death. Phaedo thus bestows on Socrates a kind of immortality, perhaps the only kind of immortality a reasonable man may hope for. Phaedo, however, is not only a narrator here but also an evangelist in the precise meaning of the word, for he brings the good news of his teacher's pious speeches and deeds on his last day to men at large. By presenting Socrates' last conversation and death through the words of Phaedo and by naming the dialogue after him, Plato suggests that Socrates intended to make philosophy appear religious to a wide audience through the evangelical activity of Phaedo and others, including perhaps Plato himself.

The *Phaedo* is the Platonic dialogue in which Socrates is executed for impiety and in which he appears to be most pious. He explains that since he has been in prison he has composed a hymn to Apollo, the ancestral god of Athens. He expresses his belief that after death his soul will dwell with the gods. And he then dies happily, thereby appearing to prove the sincerity of his belief that a blissful afterlife awaits him. Moreover, the fact that such pious behavior at this date cannot save Socrates from execution strengthens the impression that he is genuinely pious. Through his speeches and deeds on the day of his death, Socrates creates a pious image of himself that will lay to rest the charge that philosophers as such are necessarily impious men.

In addition, Socrates seeks to assuage the religious passions of his companions by arguing that the soul is immortal. Human beings, he claims, are composed of two radically distinct beings: the body and the soul. The body alone is responsible for all the ills and uncertainties that men suffer from in life. But death destroys the body, liberates the soul from the body, and enables the soul of the philosopher to ascend to the gods. Once the soul of the philosopher is liberated from the body, it is justly rewarded with the perfect wisdom that it has always longed for, and it lives forever in complete happiness. And the souls of the wicked, Socrates adds, are doomed for eternity. Socrates' argument for the immortality of the soul is deeply flawed; he himself says soon before he dies that the argument admits of many objections. Socrates' intention in making this bad argument is not to persuade his companions' reason but to charm and hence calm their religious passions. In the light of an eternal life of perfect wisdom and happiness, the uncertainty they suffer from and the injustice they witness in this life are revealed to be insignificant. By making this admittedly inadequate argument for the immortality of the soul and by dying in a way that seems to demonstrate his belief in this argument, Socrates gives Cebes and Simmias hope for the cosmic justice and perfect wisdom they long for. In the *Phaedo*, then, Socrates gives philosophy a religious cloak in order to assuage the religious passions that naked philosophy must offend.

But even as Socrates encourages his students to hope for cosmic justice and perfect wisdom, he also gives them the experience of pleasure in the midst of injustice and uncertainty. The conversation that takes place in Socrates' prison cell during the few hours before his execution is an exceedingly pleasant one. Not only do his companions laugh several times, but Socrates himself laughs, something he never does in any other Platonic dialogue. They all laugh even though they know that Socrates is about to be killed and even though they are discussing whether or not his soul will die with his body. Socrates also gives his students a history of his life that shows that his life has been pleasant despite his lack of perfect wisdom. According to his autobiographical account, Socrates' life has been marked by a series of disappointments and doubts but also by a steady progress in understanding. Through this account Socrates teaches Cebes and Simmias that the deepening awareness of one's own ignorance can lead to a continuous advancement toward wisdom. And although perfect wisdom is never attained in life, Socrates reveals that progress in wisdom can nonetheless be pleasant.

Socrates succeeded in his attempt to protect philosophers from religious persecution. After his death the opinion that philosophers were essentially impious men gradually faded away, and philosophers came to be tolerated and even admired in the political communities of the ancient world. Such students of philosophy as Scipio Africanus, Cato the Younger, and Cicero became famous and powerful statesmen. And even when the new religion of Christianity swept away the old pagan religion, the good reputation of Socrates and Plato in particular and of philosophers in general was not destroyed. Indeed, the pious image of the philosopher that Socrates presented in the *Phaedo* proved to be so appealing to the root passions of religious men that even the Christians, who rejected so much of ancient civilization, admired Socrates and Plato and sought to portray them as Christians before their time. Of course, religious persecution of individual philosophers persisted after Socrates' death, but the view that philosophy as such was a necessarily impious activity never prevailed in the post-Socratic ancient and Christian world. For after the *Phaedo* a defender of philosophers from the charge of impiety could always point to that dialogue as strong evidence that the philosopher as such is not an impious man.

Socrates, then, sought to preserve philosophy within the political community by accommodating the religious passions of that community. He did not deny that religion can do great harm to philosophers in particular and to political society as a whole. He did not even deny that philosophers should seek to temper religious fanaticism. But in his view, religious passions are so deeply embedded in human nature that the philosopher can never succeed in tempering them by challenging the authority of religion and promoting a predominantly secular society. The philosopher can succeed in moderating men's religious passions only by winning men's confidence and he can win their confidence only by assuring them that he, too, is a religious person.

Socrates would have had important disagreements with the modern political philosophers' understanding of the problem of religion, politics, and philosophy. Insofar as they sought to protect philosophy from religious persecution and to temper religious fanaticism in society at large, Socrates would have agreed with their goals. But he would have regarded as excessive their hope that a liberal, commercial society enlightened by the teachings of political philosophers would attenuate the religious passions of human beings. In Socrates' view, religious desires for cosmic justice and perfect wisdom are too powerful to be satisfied for long in such a society as our own. He would have feared that such unsatisfied religious passions would reemerge in untutored and dangerous forms in such a society. Socrates, then, would have doubted that the modern philosophers' political reform of society could succeed because he would have doubted that their psychological reform of human beings could succeed.

More importantly, Socrates would have feared that the modern philosophers' failure to appreciate the power of religious passion would lead to a corruption of philosophy itself. Socrates teaches that it is only through continuous reflection on the religious passions for justice and for certainty in his own soul that the philosopher can guard against those passions and prevent them from influencing his thinking. When modern philosophers underestimate the power of such passions, they run the risk of being unwittingly influenced by them and of exaggerating the certainty of their own teachings. Furthermore, by attempting to replace the political authority of religion with the political authority of philosophy, these philosophers would be tempted to make extreme and unjustified claims for the certainty of philosophic wisdom to others as well, including the philosophic young. And by making such extreme claims, they would run the risk of inspiring disappointment in those who had believed their claims. We see in our own day how, although the natural sciences continue to be admired for the certain knowledge they provide, it is widely doubted that political philosophy can provide any knowledge whatsoever about the proper ends of political society. The extreme pessimism about political philosophy prevalent today, which stands in such striking contrast to the optimism of earlier generations, is what Socrates would have predicted to result from early modern political philosophy's abandonment of theoretical and political moderation.

What lessons can we draw from the *Phaedo* for our understanding of the issue of religion and politics as it confronts us today? A study of this work should make us aware that the demand for a greater political role for religion poses potential dangers for both political society and political philosophy. The fears expressed by some that a religious revival in the political arena may lead to intimidation and eventually persecution of religious and nonreligious minorities are not unreasonable fears. On the other hand, the expectation that such religious demands will fade away is unreasonable, for those demands stem from powerful passions in the human soul. Our goal, then, should be to temper those powerful religious passions. But because they are so powerful, we must be willing to accommodate them, albeit with very great caution.

What would a cautious approach to the issues of religion and politics consist of? It would consist, first, of distinguishing between gentle expressions of religious passion that do not pose a direct threat to the civil peace and the rights of minorities and punitive expressions of religious passion that do pose such a threat and, then, of accommodating the former while striving to weaken the latter. The demand that prayer be allowed in the public schools, for example, reflects the desire on the part of a large majority of Americans that the government recognize the dignity of their faith. And since this demand does not entail the demand that those who do not share this faith take part in such a prayer, it poses no direct threat to religious and nonreligious minorities. It is, of course, true that prayer in the public schools might give rise to subtle forms of intimidation directed at those who choose not to pray. But the failure to accommodate such a relatively gentle demand might eventually provoke an outburst of frustrated religious passion that might, in turn, lead to open intimidation and even persecution of religious and nonreligious minorities. Allowing voluntary prayer in public schools would be a prudent way of accommodating the gentle religious passions of our people.

In contrast, the demand that abortion be banned necessarily entails the demand that those who have or who perform abortions be punished. And although this demand reflects a genuine compassion for the unborn and a concern for the sanctity of human life, it also reflects a desire to punish those who believe that abortion is not a sin and act according to their belief. The fact that violence has been connected with the antiabortion movement and not, for example, with the movement to allow prayer in the public schools also suggests that this movement is motivated, at least in part, by harsh religious passions. And since such harsh passions might lead directly to the persecution of religious and nonreligious minorities, and to civil discord as well, our goal should be to weaken them.

Recent experience has shown that unbending opposition to the antiabortion movement does not weaken or temper the passions that animate it but only serves to inflame them. Specifically, the Supreme

Court's declaration that there is a constitutional right to abortion has deeply offended those who oppose abortion and has provoked them to make the severe demand that abortion be declared unconstitutional. The only way to temper the punitive passions of the antiabortion movement, then, is by at once accommodating them to some degree and opposing them with a moral authority more powerful than the Supreme Court. We should allow the legislatures of the several states to decide whether or not abortion should be legal. Such an approach would allow those who oppose abortion to make their case directly to the people of each state. And should they fail to persuade a majority in some states— and it is likely, at present, that they would fail—they would be compelled either to abide by the majority's decision and hope to persuade it at some future date or to resort to brazenly illegal activities and thereby harm their chances of ever persuading the majority. And if they should refuse to abide by the majority's decision and resort to harassment and even to violence, the government could oppose them forcefully and effectively in the name not of the unelected judiciary but of the majority.

Such an accommodation would not entirely defuse the harsh passions of the antiabortion movement and consequently would not remove the danger of civil discord and persecution. Yet precisely because the passions animating that movement are so powerful, it would be imprudent not to accommodate them at all. Indeed, the abortion issue reflects more clearly than does the issue of prayer in the public schools the intractable nature of the problem of religion and politics as a whole: It shows that religious passions inevitably enter the political arena and that, when they do so, they inevitably threaten to foster civil discord and the persecution of religious and nonreligious minorities.

Whatever specific steps we take to achieve the goal of tempering religious passions, we should do so with the awareness that the problem of religion and politics can never be solved, since it is a permanent problem that arises out of human nature. Such an awareness should inspire in us a spirit of political moderation. It should enable us to resist both the hope that a greater political role for religion will be without dangers and the hope that the demands for such a role can be ignored or wished away. The former tempts us to relax our vigilance against excesses of religious fervor, and the latter tempts us to overlook the danger that frustrated religious passions will erupt in untutored and extreme forms.

The awareness of the power of religious passions should lead us to strive for theoretical moderation as well. It should lead us to scrutinize our own hearts lest we be led astray by our own religious passions. If Socratic philosophy teaches us anything, it teaches us that only through continuous reflection on those passions of ours—both religious and nonreligious—that lead us to distort the world can we ever hope to understand the problem of religion and politics or any other important human problems.

Contributors

PETER AHRENSDORF is visiting instructor of political science at Kenyon College and a doctoral candidate in political science at the University of Chicago. His principal interests lie in political philosophy and American political thought.

FRED E. BAUMANN was director of the Public Affairs Conference Center at Kenyon College from 1980 to 1986. Currently assistant professor of political science at Kenyon, Professor Baumann is the author of numerous works in political thought and public policy. He is editor of *Human Rights and American Foreign Policy* and *Democratic Capitalism?* and coeditor of *Crime and Punishment* and *American Defense Policy and Liberal Democracy.*

JERRY H. COMBEE is dean of the School of Business and Government at Grove City College, Grove City, Pennsylvania. The holder of a doctorate in government from Cornell University, Dr. Combee is the author of *Designed for Destiny* and *Democracy at Risk,* as well as texts used in private Christian academies. As his essay indicates, he studies the relationship of religion to modern political philosophy.

WERNER J. DANNHAUSER is professor of government at Cornell University. He is author of *Nietzsche's View of Socrates* and numerous other writings on political philosophy.

ROBERT F. DRINAN, S.J., is professor of law at the Georgetown University Law Center. Father Drinan was a member of Congress from Massachusetts from 1971 to 1981 and served as the dean of the Boston College law school from 1956 to 1970. He is the author of numerous works on religious and political matters.

FATHER ERNEST L. FORTIN is professor of theology at Boston College and a member of the Andover Newton–Boston College graduate faculty of theology. Father Fortin studies problems of Christianity and political order from the historical as well as the contemporary point of view. He has written extensively on major thinkers, most especially Augustine, Aquinas, and Dante.

KENNETH M. JENSEN taught in the Integrated Program in Humane Studies at Kenyon College from 1979 to 1981. The holder of a doctorate in Russian history, Dr. Jensen is the author of *Beyond Marx and Mach* and other works on Russian and Soviet Marxism. Coeditor of *Crime and Punishment* and *American Defense Policy and Liberal Democracy,* he is currently director of research and studies at the United States Institute of Peace.

FREDERICK SCHAUER is professor of law at the University of Michigan. He was Cutler Professor of Law at the College of William and Mary and also taught at West Virginia University. Professor Schauer is the author of *Free Speech: A Philosophical Enquiry* and, since 1983, of the annual supplements to *Gunther on Constitutional Law.* A member of the recent Attorney General's Commission on Pornography, Professor Schauer specializes in constitutional law, the First Amendment, and legal philosophy.

Index